Ross Dobson

3 ways with...

whitecap

contents

a few of my favourite things...

Raindrops on roses and whiskers on kittens are not on my list of favourite things — or that is, not when it comes to stocking the fridge and pantry. Instead, my list is full of basic, readily available ingredients that have multiple uses and have the added benefit of making my cooking life easier.

Let's face it — we all have our favourites. I have a top ten which keeps changing — depending on my mood or the season — but will almost always include tinned tomatoes and barbecued chickens. Anchovies and curry pastes. Coconut milk and feta. Dried pasta and instant polenta. Tofu and soy sauce.

And bread. Stale, of course. It isn't the best word to associate with food but let's face it, 'stale' is what happens to bread. And due to one of life's more unfortunate paradoxes, the better the bread, the quicker it stales. But don't worry — fresh bread doesn't make for good crumbing!

Your kitchen is probably already filled with many of the 100 ingredients featured in this book (they've all been in my top 10 at some time). I make no attempt to reinvent your pantry or prescribe what you *should* have in your kitchen. Instead, I'm offering you *3 ways with...* those ingredients you'll already have to hand. These base ingredients are here to act as a framework for the start of something good.

Whatever I cook I want there to be a little magic involved. A little 'I can't believe I made this'. Simplicity is the key here.

For the recipes with a short cooking time, you only want to whiz, chop, toss, fry or boil a few ingredients to make something delicious. Take the creamy artichoke soup recipe (page 91). It has four ingredients. Heat in a saucepan. Whiz in a food processor. Ready in 15 minutes. Or the white bean and tuna salad (page 103). Open a tin. Chop and toss together. Ready in 10 minutes. Done deal.

For me, it's also okay for recipes to have a long cooking time — just as long as they have next to no prep time! So don't be afraid when you see the words 'slow' and 'cooking' used together. Slow cooking is like alchemy. It's even more magical when you can prepare it quickly and leave it to do its own thing.

The important thing is don't fuss too much and you will enjoy it even more. Like the recipe for slow-cooked lamb shanks with lentils (page 131). It's actually scary how short this recipe is. It has a handful of ingredients and about 10 seconds prep time (you have to chop some pancetta). Actually, make that 20 seconds prep time (you also have to open a tin of tomatoes). Put it all in a pot for a couple of hours. Take a bath. Do a yoga class. Walk the dog. Lift the lid and voila! You won't believe you made it. This is the magic I'm talking about.

What are your favourite things? I hope you find many of them in them in the 300 recipes in this book. You don't need pictures to inspire you. Have a look in your fridge, freezer or pantry. The inspiration is there already.

Enjoy!

how it works...

The recipes in *3 ways with...* don't look like other recipes. There are no long, complicated recipes. The recipes have a casual, relaxed feel — a handful of this, a squeeze of that. Each recipe serves 4 (unless it says otherwise). The recipes don't get bogged down in detail — so neither should you.

ten steps for *3 ways with...*

1 Choose an ingredient from the list of 100 (see the next page).

2 Go to the page you need and read the three ways you have to use that ingredient.

3 Choose a recipe you like. Or...

4 ... if you are cooking for others call, email or send them a text message with their 3 options (believe me, they will be impressed at your knowledge, versatility and cooking skills).

5 Make a shopping list. This is made easy. The highlighted words in the text are the ingredients you'll need.

6 Do a quick shop — in your lunch break or on your way home. Or...

7 ... since some of the recipes are so simple, find the ingredients at home.

8 Before cooking, read the recipe again and check out all those things which make cooking easy, casual and relaxed. Things like making sure you know the cooking time, having the oven hot and ready to go, having the prepared ingredients at hand.

9 Always keep the book somewhere obvious so others can see how great it is. Or...

10 ... if you want people to believe you are a naturally versatile and really talented cook, hide this book.

the 100 ingredients

3 ways with...

ingredients from **the fridge**

bacon is also used in recipes on pages...
27, 53, 109, 137 and 181.

bacon

penne with bacon, chilli and tomato

Cook 400 g (14 oz) **penne** in boiling water for 8–10 minutes. Drain and return to the pan. Meanwhile, heat a splash of **olive oil** in a frying pan, add 4 chopped **bacon slices** and stir-fry over a high heat for a few minutes, so the bacon sizzles and crisps and flavours the oil. Add 1 chopped **onion**, 2 chopped **garlic cloves**, 2 seeded and chopped **small red chillies** and stir-fry for a few minutes, to soften the onion. Add 400 g (14 oz) tinned **chopped tomatoes** and 125 ml (4 fl oz/ $1/2$ cup) water to the pan. Bring the sauce to the boil then simmer for 10 minutes. Add the sauce to the pasta and stir to coat the pasta over a low heat for a minute to warm through. Serve with grated **parmesan**.

egg and bacon pie

Have your oven hot and ready at 220°C (425°F/Gas 7). Line a 1.5 litre (52 fl oz/6 cup) baking dish with frozen **puff pastry** and cook in the oven for 10 minutes. Cook 6–8 roughly chopped **bacon slices** in a non-stick frying pan for 5 minutes, stirring over a medium heat. Allow to cool. Place half the bacon over the baked pastry. Carefully break 8 **eggs** on top of the bacon and lightly season. Add 2 tablespoons chopped **flat-leaf (Italian) parsley** on top of the eggs and top with the remaining bacon. Bake for 20–25 minutes, until the eggs are cooked and the pastry golden. Great for winter supper with **potato mash**.

warm spinach, egg and bacon salad

Place 3–4 large handfuls **baby English spinach leaves** and 3 roughly chopped **hard-boiled eggs** in a large bowl. Heat a few splashes of **light olive oil** in a frying pan and cook 3 roughly chopped **bacon slices** for 4–5 minutes, just so the bacon starts to turn golden and crispy. Remove the pan from the heat and add 1 crushed **garlic clove**, 1 teaspoon **mild mustard** and 1 tablespoon **red wine** to the hot bacon, stirring quickly to combine. Pour all the ingredients, including the hot oil from the pan, over the spinach. Toss together, so the spinach just begins to wilt, and add some **black pepper** to serve.

bacon / fridge

barbecued chicken is also used in recipes on pages...
43, 109, 189, 199, 201 and 213.

barbecued chicken

chicken and vegetable pot pie

Have your oven hot and ready at 220°C (425°F/Gas 7). Heat 60 g (2¹/₄ oz) butter in a frying pan. When sizzling hot, add 1 chopped carrot and 2 chopped celery stalks and stir-fry for a few minutes. Add 2 tablespoons plain (all-purpose) flour and cook for 2 minutes (it should thickly coat the vegetables, but be careful not to burn the flour). Add the chopped meat from half a barbecued chicken, 80 g (2³/₄ oz/¹/₂ cup) peas and a handful of chopped flat-leaf (Italian) parsley. Stir around for a minute then add 500 ml (17 fl oz/2 cups) chicken stock and 250 ml (9 fl oz/1 cup) pouring (whipping) cream. Season well and slowly bring to the boil, stirring constantly, until slightly thickened. Spoon into an ovenproof dish and top with some puff pastry, trimmed to fit the dish, or a layer of potato mash and bake for 20–25 minutes, until the pastry is golden.

tex-mex chicken salad

Mash 1 avocado in a bowl with 125 g (4¹/₂ oz/¹/₂ cup) sour cream and 2 tablespoons lemon juice and season well. Put the shredded meat and skin of a barbecued chicken in a bowl with 1 red onion sliced into thin wedges, 2 large tomatoes, chopped into bite-sized pieces, 1 handful pitted black olives, 1 large handful chopped coriander (cilantro) leaves and stems, 3 tablespoons jalapeño chillies (in brine) and 3–4 handfuls shredded iceberg lettuce. Toss to combine and top with dollops of the avocado dressing. Serve in warm taco shells.

chinatown chicken and watercress salad

Cut the meat and skin of a barbecued chicken into thin strips. Put in a bowl with 250 g (9 oz) halved cherry tomatoes, 1 large handful roughly chopped coriander (cilantro) leaves, 3 thinly sliced spring onions (scallions) and 200 g (7 oz) watercress, leaves picked. Toss gently to combine. Combine 2 tablespoons light soy sauce, 2 tablespoons rice vinegar, 1 teaspoon sugar, 1 teaspoon sesame oil and 1 teaspoon grated ginger in a bowl. Pour over the salad to serve.

barbecued chicken / fridge

beer

steak, onion and ale casserole

Have your oven hot and ready at 160°C (315°F/Gas 2–3). Chop 1 kg (2 lb 4 oz) **chuck** or **stewing steak** into large bite-sized pieces and toss around in a bowl with 60 g (2¹/₄ oz/¹/₂ cup) **plain (all-purpose) flour**, 1 teaspoon **sea salt** and ¹/₂ teaspoon **white pepper**. Heat a splash of **olive oil** and 40 g (1¹/₂ oz) **butter** in a large ovenproof saucepan and cook the beef in 2 batches for 2–3 minutes, to gently sizzle and turn brown. Put the browned beef in a bowl. Add 4 peeled and quartered **onions** to the pan and cook for 8–10 minutes, stirring often, so the onions soften and turn golden. Return the beef to the pan with 350 ml (12 fl oz) **ale** or **beer**, 1 litre (35 fl oz/4 cups) **beef stock** and 2 **bay leaves**. Boil, stirring once or twice, then cover with a piece of crumpled baking paper and cook in the oven for 2 hours. Remove and cook on a rapid simmer for 20 minutes, so the sauce is thick and glossy. Serve with **potato mash**.

slow braised lamb shank and vegetable hotpot

Have your oven hot and ready at 160°C (315°F/Gas 2–3). Heat a splash of **olive oil** in a casserole dish and cook 1 chopped **onion** and 2 chopped **garlic cloves** in the oil for 2–3 minutes, so the onion gently softens and sizzles. Add 375 ml (13 fl oz/1¹/₂ cups) **beer**, 250 ml (9 fl oz/1 cup) **chicken stock** and a splash of **worcestershire sauce** to the pan and bring to the boil. Add 4 trimmed **lamb shanks**, place a tight-fitting lid on the dish and cook in the oven for 1¹/₂ hours. Remove from the oven and turn the lamb shanks, basting in the gravy. Add 2 peeled and quartered **large potatoes** and 2 chopped **carrots**, season well and return to the oven for 1 hour. Stir through a handful of roughly chopped **flat-leaf (Italian) parsley** and serve.

sweet and sour tapas chorizo

Stir-fry 1 finely chopped **red onion** in 1 tablespoon **olive oil** for a few minutes, so the onion sizzles and softens. Add 1 tablespoon **soft brown sugar** and 1 sliced **chorizo** and cook for 2–3 minutes, so the sausage slices start to brown. Add 400 g (14 oz) tinned **cannellini beans**, rinsed and drained, 125 ml (4 fl oz/¹/₂ cup) **beer**, 3 tablespoons **red wine vinegar** and 1 **bay leaf** to the pan and boil for 6–8 minutes, until almost all the liquid has evaporated. Serve as a shared starter with warm **bread**.

black olives are also used in recipes on pages...
15, 31, 43, 55, 101, 103, 105, 161, 181, 191, 207 and 209.

black olives

herby olive sauce

Blend 185 g (6½ oz/1½ cups) pitted black olives, 1 small handful each flat-leaf (Italian) parsley and basil, 1 tablespoon oregano and a good squeeze of lemon juice in a food processor until you have a chunky paste. With the motor running, slowly pour in 3 tablespoons good fruity olive oil. Keep in a bowl and taste for seasoning. Serve with chargrilled octopus or spoon onto barbecued lamb cutlets.

olive and roasted cherry tomato pasta sauce

Have your oven hot and ready at 180°C (350°F/Gas 4). Put 500 g (1 lb 2 oz) cherry tomatoes in a bowl with 3 tablespoons light olive oil, 2 chopped garlic cloves, 1 bay leaf, 2 teaspoons oregano, 1 teaspoon sea salt and a pinch of sugar. Toss around in the bowl a few times and put all the ingredients on a baking tray and cook in the oven for 30 minutes. Remove from the oven and allow to cool on the tray for the flavours to intensify. Cook 400 g (14 oz) of your favourite pasta (long varieties go well with this sauce). Put the tomatoes in a saucepan with 60 g (2¼ oz/½ cup) pitted black olives and heat through. Spoon the sauce over the pasta and serve with grated parmesan.

penne with olives, tuna and chilli herbs

Cook 400 g (14 oz) penne in boiling water for 8–10 minutes. Drain and return to the warm pan. Meanwhile, cook 1 sliced red onion, 2 seeded and chopped small red chillies and 2 chopped garlic cloves in 3 tablespoons light olive oil for 4–5 minutes, so the onion gently sizzles and softens in the oil. Add 185 g (6½ oz) tinned tuna to the pan with a handful each chopped basil, mint and flat-leaf (Italian) parsley and stir around over a gentle heat to warm the tuna through, but not breaking up too much. Add to the pasta and gently heat for 2–3 minutes. Season well and serve.

blue cheese is also used in recipes on pages...
41 and 91.

blue cheese

blue cheese and broad bean risotto

Simmer 750 ml (26 fl oz/3 cups) chicken stock. Cook 1 chopped small onion and 1 chopped garlic clove in a splash of olive oil, so the onion gently sizzles and softens and turns opaque. Add 110 g (3³/4 oz/¹/2 cup) arborio or risotto rice, stir for 1 minute then add 125 ml (4 fl oz/¹/2 cup) of the stock to the saucepan, stirring until the rice has absorbed almost all the liquid. Repeat until all the stock is in the pan and the rice is soft but has a little bite in the centre. Stir through 3 tablespoons crumbled blue cheese, 20 g (³/4 oz) butter and 95 g (3¹/4 oz/¹/2 cup) blanched and peeled broad beans. Season well and serve this rich risotto as a starter.

blue cheese and peach salad

Put 1 bunch frisée, washed and trimmed (or 3–4 large handfuls of mixed salad leaf) in a large bowl. In a small bowl combine 2 teaspoons sherry vinegar or white wine vinegar, 2 tablespoons olive oil, 1 teaspoon dijon mustard and black pepper. Add 2–3 sliced peaches to the salad, pour over the dressing and toss to combine. Top the salad with 3 tablespoons crumbled blue cheese and serve.

blue cheese and walnut pizza with pear and rocket salad

Have your oven hot and ready at 200°C (400°F/Gas 6). Place a frozen pizza base on a baking tray and into the oven for 10 minutes. Remove, brush with a little olive oil and top each pizza with 150 g (5¹/2 oz/1 cup) crumbled blue cheese and 125 g (4¹/2 oz/1 cup) roughly chopped walnuts. Return to the oven for about 8 minutes, so the cheese is gooey and the walnuts are slightly golden. Remove the pizza and top with 2 handfuls baby rocket (arugula) leaves, half a sliced firm brown pear, a good grinding of black pepper and a drizzling of olive oil. Cut into wedges and serve. Serves 2.

cheddar is also used in recipes on pages...
37, 143 and 187.

cheddar

chicken and leek pasta

Cook 400 g (14 oz) **small shell pasta** in boiling water for 8–10 minutes. Drain well and return to the saucepan. Heat 60 g (2 1/4 oz) **butter** in a saucepan. When the butter sizzles, add 1 finely sliced **leek** and stir-fry for a few minutes, until soft and silky. Add 2 cubed **boneless, skinless chicken breasts** and stir-fry for 5 minutes, so the chicken starts to turn golden. Add 2 tablespoons **plain (all-purpose) flour** and cook for 1 minute, stirring constantly (it should look like a thick paste coating the leeks) and gradually pour in 500 ml (17 fl oz/2 cups) **milk**. Cook on a gentle heat, stirring constantly, until thick and smooth. Add 125 g (4 1/2 oz/1 cup) grated **cheddar**, 50 g (1 3/4 oz/ 1/2 cup) grated **parmesan** and stir until the cheese has melted. Stir through the pasta and spoon into a large serving dish. Sprinkle with more **cheddar** and **parmesan** and cook under a hot grill (broiler) until the top is golden and crisp.

really cheesy cauliflower

Have your oven hot and ready at 180°C (350°F/Gas 4). Break 8 large pieces off a head of **cauliflower** and cook in boiling water for 5 minutes. Drain and place the pieces to fit snugly in a baking dish. Put 250 ml (9 fl oz/1 cup) **pouring (whipping) cream**, 1 tablespoon **plain (all-purpose) flour** and 2 teaspoons **mild mustard** in a saucepan and gently heat, stirring constantly until smooth. Add 125 g (4 1/2 oz/1 cup) grated **cheddar** to the pan, stir around until the cheese has just melted then pour over the cauliflower pieces. Sprinkle 60 g (2 1/4 oz/1/2 cup) extra grated **cheddar** on top and bake for 30 minutes.

tuna casserole

Have your oven hot and ready at 180°C (350°F/Gas 4). Combine 370 g (13 oz) tinned **tuna**, drained of excess oil, 250 g (9 oz/1 cup) **sour cream**, 125 g (4 1/2 oz/1 cup) grated **cheddar**, 125 ml (4 fl oz/ 1/2 cup) **milk**, 1 tablespoon **cornflour (cornstarch)** and 3 chopped **spring onions (scallions)** in a bowl. Spoon into a 1.5 litre (52 fl oz/6 cup) ceramic baking dish, top with 60 g (4 1/2 oz/1/2 cup) grated **cheddar**, sprinkle with **paprika** and cook in the oven for 40 minutes.

cheddar / fridge

chorizo is also used in recipes on pages...
17, III and 131.

chorizo

paprika risoni hotpot

Cook 1 chopped **red onion**, 1 chopped **garlic clove** and 1 chopped **chorizo** in a splash of **olive oil** for 5 minutes, so the onion sizzles in the oil and to release all the hidden spices in the sausage. Add ¹/₂ teaspoon **smoked paprika** and 200 g (7 oz/1 cup) **risoni**, and stir to coat the risoni in the spicy pan juices. Add 400 g (14 oz) tinned **chopped tomatoes** and 500 ml (17 fl oz/2 cups) **chicken stock** and bring to the boil. Place on a tight-fitting lid and cook over a very low heat for 20 minutes. Remove from the heat and leave the lid on for a further 5 minutes. Remove, stir through a handful of chopped **flat-leaf (Italian) parsley**, and serve hot.

spanish minestrone

Heat a generous splash of **olive oil** in a saucepan and stir-fry 1 chopped **onion** with 1 finely cubed **chorizo** for 4–5 minutes on a medium heat, to soften the onion and bring out all the spices in the sausage. Add 500 ml (17 fl oz/2 cups) **chicken stock**, 400 g (14 oz) tinned **chopped tomatoes**, 400 g (14 oz) tinned **cannellini beans**, rinsed and drained, and 1 finely cubed **potato**. Bring to the boil and simmer for 15 minutes, until the potato is nicely soft. Stir through a handful of roughly chopped **flat-leaf (Italian) parsley** and serve topped with some crumbled **feta** or **manchego cheese**.

chorizo and seafood gumbo

Cook 12 **raw prawns (shrimp)** in a splash of **light olive oil** for 2 minutes each side, so they turn pink and flavour the oil. Remove from the pan. Add 1 chopped **chorizo**, 1 chopped **onion**, 1 small cubed **green capsicum (pepper)**, 2 sliced **celery stalks** and ¹/₂ teaspoon each **cayenne pepper** and **black pepper** to the pan and cook for 5 minutes. Add 1 litre (35 fl oz/4 cups) **chicken stock** and 3 tablespoons **medium-grain rice** and boil for 20–25 minutes, so the rice is really soft. Return the prawns to the pan with 300 g (10¹/₂ oz) bite-sized cubes of **white fish fillet** and 12 **mussels**. Stir around to coat the seafood in the gumbo, cover and simmer for 10 minutes, so the fish turns white and the mussels open. Serve in large bowls.

cream cheese

creamy potato and leek soup

Cook 2 sliced **leeks** in 40 g (1¹/₂ oz) gently sizzling **butter** for a few minutes, until soft and silky. Add 2 litres (70 fl oz/8 cups) **chicken stock**, 2 peeled and cubed **large all-purpose potatoes** and cook on a rapid simmer for 10 minutes, so the potatoes soften but don't break up. Reduce the heat to really low and stir through 125 g (4¹/₂ oz/ ¹/₂ cup) **cream cheese**, a handful of finely chopped **flat-leaf (Italian) parsley**, a tablespoon of snipped **chives** and some **black pepper**. Cook on a gentle heat for a few more minutes. Serve with **buttered toast** on the side.

fettucine boscaiola

Cook 2 **bacon slices** and 1 chopped **onion** in a small splash of **olive oil** for 4–5 minutes. Add 180 g (6¹/₂ oz/2 cups) sliced **button mushrooms** and 1 chopped **garlic clove** and stir-fry for 2–3 minutes, to soften the mushrooms. Chop a 300 g (10¹/₂ oz) block of **cream cheese** into 8 cubes and add to the pan. Stir over a gentle heat until the cream cheese has melted evenly. Remove from the heat and cover to keep warm. Meanwhile, cook 400 g (14 oz) **fettucine** in boiling water for 8–10 minutes. Drain well and return to the warm pan with the sauce and 50 g (1³/₄ oz/¹/₂ cup) grated **parmesan** and a good grinding of **black pepper**. Stir to coat the pasta in the sauce. Top with extra **parmesan** and serve.

cream cheese and cherry danish

Have your oven hot and ready at 220°C (425°F/Gas 7). Line a baking tray with baking paper. Cut a sheet of **puff pastry** into four equal squares and place on the baking tray. Put a tablespoon of **cream cheese** in the centre of each square with a tablespoon of **cherry jam** (or your favourite) on top. Bring the four points of the pastry towards the centre and pinch or twist firmly. Don't worry if there are little gaps in the pastry. The cheese and jam will leak out and look gooey and yummy. Bake for 20 minutes, until puffed and golden. Allow to cool before lightly dusting with **icing (confectioners') sugar**. Serve with **coffee** for brunch, or hot with **ice cream** for dessert.

egg noodles

yum cha noodles

Cook 300 g (10¹/₂ oz) **fresh Chinese egg noodles** in boiling water for 2 minutes (or 3–4 minutes if using dried). Rinse under cold water, drain really well and toss the noodles around in a bowl with 2 teaspoons **sesame oil**. Heat 2 tablespoons **vegetable oil** in a hot wok. Add 1 chopped **garlic clove**, 2 teaspoons grated **ginger**, 125 g (4¹/₂ oz/1 cup) **garlic chives**, cut into 3 cm (1¹/₄ inch) lengths, and 180 g (6¹/₂ oz/2 cups) **bean sprouts** for a minute, just so the vegetables wilt. Add the noodles to the wok and stir-fry for 2–3 minutes. Add 2 tablespoons **light soy sauce** and 2 tablespoons **oyster sauce** to the wok and stir-fry for 2 minutes, ensuring all the noodles are evenly coated in the sauce. Serve spinkled with 1 tablespoon lightly toasted **sesame seeds**.

a short long soup

Cook 300 g (10¹/₂ oz) **fresh Chinese egg noodles** in boiling water for 2 minutes (or 3–4 minutes if using dried) and drain. Boil 1 litre (35 fl oz/4 cups) **chicken stock** with a splash of **light soy sauce** to season. Add 200 g (7 oz/1 cup) sliced **Chinese barbecued pork (char siu)** and 1 bunch roughly chopped **Chinese broccoli (gai larn)** to the pot and cook for 2 minutes, so the greens turn emerald and soften. Put the noodles into serving bowls and spoon over the hot soup mixture. Top with sliced **spring onions (scallions)** and a drizzling of **sesame oil**.

cold tossed noodle salad

Put 2 tablespoons **dried shrimp** (available from the Asian section at supermarkets) in a bowl and cover with boiling water for 10 minutes. Drain well and finely chop. Cook 300 g (10¹/₂ oz) **fresh Chinese egg noodles** in boiling water for 2 minutes (or 3–4 minutes if using dried) and drain. Combine 3 tablespoons **light soy sauce**, 2 tablespoons **rice vinegar**, 2 teaspoons finely grated **ginger**, 2 teaspoons **sesame oil** and a good pinch of **sugar** in a small bowl. Pour over the noodles and add the chopped shrimp. Toss around for a minute to really coat the noodles in the dressing. Finely slice a **small carrot**, a **small red capsicum (pepper)** and 4 **spring onions (scallions)** and add to the noodles with 1 large handful **coriander (cilantro) leaves**, roughly chopped, and toss well.

feta is also used in recipes on pages...
25, 63, 67, 91, 97, 99, 107, 123 and 131.

feta

artichoke, orange and feta salad

Cut 6 tinned and drained **artichokes** in half and put in a bowl with 2 peeled and segmented **oranges**, 1 finely sliced **red onion**, 1 large handful each **flat-leaf (Italian) parsley** and **mint**, 140 g (5 oz/ 1 cup) cubed **marinated feta** and 80 g (2³/4 oz/¹/2 cup) pitted **kalamata olives**. Combine 2 tablespoons good **olive oil** in a bowl with 1 tablespoon **red wine vinegar**, 1 crushed **garlic clove** and **salt** and **black pepper**. Pour the dressing over the salad and gently toss to combine. Serve with **grilled swordfish** or **tuna steaks**.

creamy feta salad dressing

Put 225 g (8 oz/1¹/2 cups) crumbled **feta** in a food processor with 2 crushed **garlic cloves**, 1 tablespoon chopped **dill** and 3 tablespoons **olive oil**. With the motor running, slowly add 185 ml (6 fl oz/³/4 cup) **milk** in a steady stream to form a thick and smooth dressing. Serve dollops over **grilled lamb** or **vegetables**.

prawns with feta

Cut 4 ripe and tasty **tomatoes** in half, squeeze out as many seeds as you can and roughly chop. Heat 2–3 tablespoons of good **fruity olive oil** in a hot frying pan and add 1 chopped **onion** and 1 chopped **garlic clove**, stirring around for 2–3 minutes to soften the onion and flavour the oil. Add the tomatoes, 1 teaspoon **dried oregano** and a small handful of roughly chopped **flat-leaf (Italian) parsley** to the pan. Cook for 2–3 minutes so the tomatoes really sizzle. Add 16 peeled and deveined **raw prawns (shrimp)** to the pan and cook for 5 minutes, so the prawns turn pink and curly. Add 3 tablespoons water and boil for a few minutes. Stir through 150 g (5¹/2 oz/1 cup) roughly crumbled **feta** and serve as a meal with **rice** or as a shared tapas dish with **bread**.

firm tofu is also used in recipes on pages...
93, 125 and 195.

firm tofu

three ways with

tofu and zucchini omelette

Stir-fry 1 grated **zucchini (courgette)** in a splash of **vegetable oil** in a non-stick frying pan for 2–3 minutes. Add 2 handfuls **baby English spinach leaves** and a few splashes of **light soy sauce** to the pan cook for 2–3 minutes, so the spinach wilts. Put 185 g (6¹/₂ oz/ 1 cup) cubed **firm tofu** over the spinach. Beat 3 **eggs** and pour into the pan and cook on a high heat for 2–3 minutes, so the edges start to puff up. Place under a hot grill (broiler) until golden and firm. Serve the omelette topped with a drizzle of **oyster sauce** and some **white pepper**. Serves 2.

chinatown mushroom and tofu stir-fry

Cut a 300 g (10¹/₂ oz) block of **firm tofu** into 16 small pieces. Have a wok hot and ready to go. Add 125 ml (4 fl oz/¹/₂ cup) **light cooking oil** to the wok. When the oil is shimmering, add the tofu pieces and fry for 3–4 minutes, until just starting to turn golden. Leaving the tofu, drain all but a tablespoon of oil from the wok. Add 2 sliced **spring onions (scallions)** and 2 teaspoons grated **ginger** and stir-fry for a few seconds, then add 500 g (1 lb 2 oz) **mixed Asian mushrooms** (try shiitake, shimeji, oyster, enoki and maybe even some swiss browns, all ends trimmed off if need be) and stir-fry for 3–4 minutes. Just when the mushrooms turn limp, add 3 tablespoons **oyster sauce** and 1 tablespoon **soy sauce**. Stir-fry to coat all the ingredients in the sauce and serve.

braised tofu in ginger, spring onion and oyster sauce

Cut a 600 g (1 lb 5 oz) block of **firm tofu** into 3 cm (1¹/₄ inch) cubes and place on paper towel. Heat 250 ml (9 fl oz/1 cup) **vegetable oil** in a wok. Cook half the tofu pieces in the hot oil for 5–6 minutes, turning often, so they sizzle and become golden. Remove to a plate, then cook the remaining tofu. Drain the oil from the wok. Return all the tofu to the wok with 250 ml (9 fl oz/ 1 cup) **chicken stock**, 2 tablespoons **oyster sauce**, 2 teaspoons **cornflour (cornstarch)**, 4–6 thin slices of **ginger**, 1 chopped **garlic clove** and 4 **spring onions (scallions)**, chopped into 4 cm (1¹/₂ inch) lengths, and bring to the boil, stirring constantly. Turn the tofu pieces over in the thickened sauce, cook for 2 minutes and serve with **rice**.

firm tofu / fridge

33

green olives are also used in recipes on pages...
183 and 207.

green olives

roasted chicken with green olives, balsamic and capers

Have your oven hot and ready at 180°C (350°F/Gas 4). Season 4 **chicken legs and thighs** with **sea salt** and **black pepper**. Heat 3 tablespoons **light olive oil** in a heavy-based frying pan. Cook half the chicken in the hot oil for 3–4 minutes each side, so the pieces are golden and the skin looks crispy. Repeat with the remaining chicken and place all the chicken in a flat baking dish. Pour 125 ml (4 fl oz/^{1}/$_2$ cup) **balsamic vinegar** over the chicken pieces and add 175 g (6 oz/1 cup) **green olives** and 1 tablespoon rinsed **baby capers**. Cook in the oven for 1 hour, turning the chicken every 20 minutes. Serve with a handful of chopped **flat-leaf (Italian) parsley** and 3 tablespoons lightly toasted **flaked almonds**. Serve with crispy **roast potatoes**.

orange and olive salad

Whisk together 125 g (4^1/$_2$ oz/ ^{1}/$_2$ cup) good **mayonnaise** with 2 tablespoons **sherry vinegar** (or any light vinegar) and 2 teaspoons finely chopped **tarragon**. Arrange 1 roughly chopped **cos (romaine) lettuce** on a plate and top with 2 peeled and finely sliced **oranges**, 1 finely sliced **red onion**, 175 g (6 oz/ 1 cup) **green olives**, 2 tablespoons rinsed **capers** and 6–8 **anchovy fillets**. Pour the dressing over the salad and serve as a starter or side to a main.

turkish olive and walnut salad

Pit and halve 350 g (12 oz/2 cups) **green olives** and toss the olives around in a bowl with 125 g (4^1/$_2$ oz/1 cup) roughly chopped **walnuts**, 1 finely sliced **red onion** and a large handful of chopped **flat-leaf (Italian) parsley**. Mix together 3 tablespoons good **fruity olive oil**, 1 tablespoon **balsamic vinegar**, ^{1}/$_2$ teaspoon **chilli flakes** and ^{1}/$_2$ teaspoon **caster (superfine) sugar**. Pour over the salad and toss once more. This salad is great with **spicy lamb meatballs, hummus** and warm Middle Eastern flat breads.

ham is also used in recipes on pages...
147 and 209.

ham

baked macaroni cheese with ham

Have your oven hot and ready at 180°C (350°F/Gas 4). Cook 400 g (14 oz) macaroni in boiling water for 8–10 minutes. Drain and return to the pan. Heat 40 g (1¹/2 oz) butter in a saucepan until it sizzles then stir in 2 tablespoons plain (all-purpose) flour over a low heat for 1 minute, until you have a smooth paste. Slowly add 500 ml (17 fl oz/2 cups) milk to the pan. You can turn the heat up here, but don't let the milk boil. Stir until you have a smooth sauce, a bit like thin custard. Add 60 g (2¹/4 oz/¹/2 cup) grated cheddar and 75 g (2¹/2 oz/¹/2 cup) grated mozzarella and stir over a low heat until the cheese has melted smoothly. Add the cheese sauce to the cooked macaroni with 155 g (5¹/2 oz/1 cup) finely sliced ham then stir around and pour into a large ceramic baking dish. Sprinkle with 60 g (2¹/4 oz/¹/2 cup) grated cheddar and cook in the oven for 25–30 minutes, until golden on top.

croque madame

Sandwich some sliced ham between 2 slices of buttered white bread which has been smeared with a mild mustard. Heat a little butter in a non-stick frying pan and cook the sandwich for 2 minutes each side, until nicely golden. Place some thinly sliced tasty cheese on top (try an aged cheddar or tasty gruyère) and place under the grill (broiler) until the cheese is bubbly and golden. Fry an egg, sunny side up, in some good olive oil and slide the egg on top of the croque. Enjoy for brunch or supper. Serves 1.

ham, mushroom and mozzarella pizza

Have your oven hot and ready at 220°C (425°F/Gas 7). Place a baking tray (or better yet, a pizza stone) in the oven to really heat up. Defrost a frozen pizza base and evenly spread with 3 tablespoons tomato passata (puréed tomatoes). Top with 155 g (5¹/2 oz/1 cup) sliced ham, 90 g (3¹/4 oz/1 cup) thinly sliced mushrooms, 1 sliced small onion and 150 g (5¹/2 oz/1 cup) grated mozzarella. You can add a sprinkling of dried herbs if you like. Place on the heated baking tray and cook for 10–15 minutes, or until the bottom of the pizza is dark golden and the cheese bubbly hot. Serves 2.

ham / fridge

lasagne sheets

tomato and spinach lasagne

Have your oven hot and ready at 180°C (350°F/Gas 4). Heat 40 g (1½ oz) **butter** in a saucepan. When it sizzles, add 2 tablespoons **plain (all-purpose) flour** and stir off the heat for a minute, until it's a thick paste. Return to the heat and gradually pour in 500 ml (17 fl oz/2 cups) **milk**, whisking all the while over a medium heat, until you have a smooth sauce, a bit like a thick custard. Stir through 150 g (5½ oz/1 cup) grated **mozzarella** and set aside. Line the bottom of a 2–2.5 litre (70–87 fl oz/ 8–10 cup) baking dish with **fresh lasagne sheets**. Top with 125 g (4½ oz) defrosted frozen **English spinach**, 2 thinly sliced **tomatoes** and a third of the sauce. Repeat once more, finishing with a layer of lasagne and the remaining sauce. Sprinkle over 50 g (1¾ oz/ ½ cup) grated **parmesan** and bake for 40 minutes, until golden.

hand-cut pasta with nutty sage butter

Roll up each of the **fresh lasagne sheets** from a 375 g (13 oz) packet into logs and slice each into 2 cm (¾ inch) wide strips. Cook in boiling water for a few minutes, until they rise to the top. Drain and return to the warm pan. Heat 60 g (2¼ oz) **butter** in a frying pan and, when it is sizzling and frothy, add 80 g (2¾ oz/½ cup) **pine nuts** and 4–6 **sage leaves** to the pan. Shake the pan over the heat until the nuts and butter are golden. Add to the pasta with 50 g (1¾ oz/½ cup) grated **parmesan**, then toss together with **sea salt** and **black pepper**.

zucchini and ricotta cannelloni

Have your oven hot and ready at 200°C (400°F/Gas 6). Cook 2 grated **zucchini (courgettes)** and 2 chopped **garlic cloves** in a splash of **olive oil** for 4–5 minutes, so the zucchini sizzles and softens. Remove to a bowl and add 500 g (1 lb 2 oz/2 cups) **ricotta** and 1 handful **flat-leaf (Italian) parsley**, chopped. Season well and stir to evenly combine. Take 2 **fresh lasagne sheets** and cut across the width to give 4 pieces. Divide the ricotta mixture between the sheets of pasta and roll up to form 4 large logs. Place the logs to fit snugly in a buttered ceramic dish. Pour over 250 ml (9 fl oz/1 cup) **tomato-based pasta sauce**, sprinkle with 50 g (1¾ oz/½ cup) grated **parmesan** and bake for 30 minutes.

mascarpone is also used in a recipe on page...
151.

mascarpone

mascarpone and gorgonzola linguine

Cook 300 g (10½ oz) linguine in boiling water for 8–10 minutes then drain well. Meanwhile, heat 110 g (3¾ oz/½ cup) mascarpone in a frying pan, stirring over a gentle heat, until warm. Stir through 75 g (2½ oz/½ cup) crumbled gorgonzola or blue cheese and a light splash of milk and stir until the cheese is melted smoothly into the warm cream. Add the sauce to the pasta and serve as a starter sprinkled with 1 tablespoon lightly toasted and chopped walnuts.

espresso mousse

Whisk 3 egg whites and 3 tablespoons caster (superfine) sugar in a bowl until firmly peaking. Add 250 ml (9 fl oz/1 cup) pouring (whipping) cream and beat until thick and creamy. Add 110 g (3¾ oz/½ cup) mascarpone and 4 tablespoons cold espresso coffee and beat until well combined. Spoon the mixture into a bowl and chill. Top with 3 tablespoons toasted flaked almonds.

orange maple mascarpone

Separate 2 eggs and beat the whites to stiff peaks. Beat the yolks with 220 g (7¾ oz/1 cup) mascarpone, 2 tablespoons maple syrup and 2 teaspoons finely grated orange zest for a few minutes until smooth and a little thickened. Fold through the egg whites. Serve with a fruit salad, grilled peaches or as a dip for fresh figs.

mayonnaise is also used in recipes on pages...
35, 161, 189 and 213.

mayonnaise

anchovy and caper mayonnaise

Put 250 g (9 oz/1 cup) good-quality mayonnaise in a food processor with 6–8 anchovy fillets and 1 teaspoon of oil from the anchovies, 1 crushed garlic clove and 1 tablespoon rinsed capers and blend for 10 seconds. Put in a bowl and stir through 2 tablespoons finely chopped flat-leaf (Italian) parsley. Add some black pepper and a squeeze of lemon juice. Serve a generous dollop with pan-fried veal cutlets or as a salad dressing.

asian coleslaw

Combine 125 g (4^{1}/$_2$ oz/^{1}/$_2$ cup) mayonnaise, 2 tablespoons rice vinegar, 1 teaspoon mild mustard and 2 teaspoons sesame oil in a bowl and stir until smooth. Combine 180 g (6^{1}/$_2$ oz/4 cups) finely shredded Chinese cabbage, 1 grated carrot, 130 g (4^3/$_4$ oz/ 1 cup) grated daikon, 4 finely sliced spring onions (scallions), and 2 handfuls chopped coriander (cilantro) leaves and stems in a large bowl. Add the mayonnaise to the salad and toss well to evenly combine.

chicken mayonnaise salad

Shred the meat and skin of a barbecued chicken and put in a bowl with 2 sliced celery stalks, 1 tablespoon rinsed capers, 70 g (2^{1}/$_2$ oz/^{1}/$_2$ cup) halved pitted black olives, 1 handful chopped flat-leaf (Italian) parsley, 2 chopped hard-boiled eggs and 250 g (9 oz/1 cup) mayonnaise. Toss to evenly combine the ingredients. Serve the salad with lightly toasted rye bread.

mozzarella is also used in recipes on pages...
37, 39 and 99.

mozzarella

mozzarella and prosciutto tortilla

Sprinkle 150 g (5^1/$_2$ oz/1 cup) grated mozzarella over a soft tortilla or burrito and lay 3–4 thin slices of prosciutto and a small handful of basil on top. Generously grind over some black pepper and place another tortilla or burrito on top. Heat a non-stick frying pan to high and cook the tortilla or burrito for 2–3 minutes each side, until golden and crisp. Cut into wedges and serve. Serves 1.

tomato, pesto and mozzarella pizza

Have your oven hot and ready at 220°C (425°F/Gas 7). Spread 1 tablespoon good-quality pesto on a small, round Greek or Egyptian bread and top with 1 sliced tomato and 6 thin slices of mozzarella. Grind over some black pepper and place on a tray and into the oven for 10 minutes. Top with some basil and a drizzle of olive oil. Serves 1.

asparagus and mozzarella omelette

Cut the ends off a bunch of asparagus and cut each spear into 3 cm (1^1/$_4$ inch) lengths. Heat a splash of olive oil in a non-stick frying pan and stir-fry the asparagus for 2–3 minutes. Have your grill (broiler) hot and ready. Beat 3 eggs in a bowl and add 75 g (2^1/$_2$ oz/^{1}/$_2$ cup) cubed mozzarella and the asparagus and season well with sea salt and black pepper. Heat 1 tablespoon olive oil in a small non-stick frying pan, swirling the pan around to coat in the oil, and pour the egg mixture evenly into the pan. Sprinkle with 3 tablespoons grated parmesan and cook for 3–4 minutes, so the edges puff, and place under the grill (broiler) and cook until golden on top. Serves 1.

parmesan is also used in recipes on pages...
13, 19, 23, 27, 39, 45, 55, 71, 79, 81, 87, 89, 91, 93, 107,
149, 159, 173, 175, 193 and 197.

parmesan

nutty red pesto

Put 1 red capsicum (pepper) over an open gas flame for 8–10 minutes, turning often so it evenly blackens (or put it on a baking tray and blast it in a really hot oven until blistered all over). Put in a plastic bag for a few minutes to cool. Peel off the skin, discard the seeds and place the flesh in a food processor with 80 g (2 3/4 oz/1/2 cup) lightly toasted cashews, 3 tablespoons lightly toasted pine nuts, 1 seeded small red chilli (optional), 3 tablespoons olive oil, a really good squeeze of lemon juice and sea salt and black pepper. Blend to a paste and remove to a bowl, then stir through a generous serve of grated parmesan.

parmesan and garlic spaghetti

Place 4 tablespoons good fruity olive oil and 4 chopped garlic cloves in a frying pan over a gentle heat. As soon as the garlic starts to sizzle, remove from the heat and allow to rest and soften in the pan, intensely flavouring the oil. Cook 400 g (14 oz) spaghetti (or other thin pasta such as linguine) in boiling water for 8–10 minutes. Drain well and return to the warm pan. Add the garlic oil and 50 g (1 3/4 oz/1/2 cup) grated parmesan and season well with sea salt and black pepper. Toss around well to combine the flavours. Enjoy as a tasty starter.

chilli parmesan asparagus

Boil some water in a frying pan and cook 350 g (12 oz) asparagus, trimmed, in the boiling water for 2 minutes. Drain well and return the asparagus to the warm pan with 40 g (1 1/2 oz) butter, 3 tablespoons breadcrumbs, 1/2 teaspoon chilli flakes and a good grinding of black pepper. Shake the pan for a few minutes so the butter melts and the crumbs turn an even golden colour. Sprinkle over 3 tablespoons finely grated parmesan and place under a hot grill (broiler) for just a minute or two until the parmesan starts to turn golden. Serve as a starter or a side dish.

parmesan / fridge

ricotta is also used in recipes on pages...
39, 71, 81, 87, 91, 167 and 173.

ricotta

three ways with

herb and chilli ricotta

Put 500 g (1 lb 2 oz/2 cups) ricotta in a food processor with 1 teaspoon chilli flakes, 3 tablespoons roughly chopped flat-leaf (Italian) parsley, 2 tablespoons roughly chopped dill, 2 teaspoons grated lemon zest, 2 tablespoons snipped chives and a generous amount of sea salt and black pepper (ricotta really needs a good seasoning). Combine until smooth, but don't over-mix. You still want to see the nice fresh flecks of herbs. Spoon into 4 individual serving cups, cover and chill until needed. Enjoy as a starter with garlic bread or toss through pasta.

ricotta, tomato and basil pasta salad

Put 4 chopped ripe and tasty tomatoes in a large bowl with 3 tablespoons good fruity olive oil, 2 crushed garlic cloves, a large handful of torn basil, 1 teaspoon sea salt and a good pinch of sugar, toss around to combine and set aside for 20 minutes, to allow the flavours to develop. Meanwhile, cook 400 g (14 oz) penne in boiling water for 8–10 minutes. Drain well. Add the pasta to the tomatoes with 250 g (9 oz/1 cup) fresh ricotta, tossing well to really combine all the flavours. Add some freshly ground black pepper and serve.

ricotta and winter green pasta sauce

Heat 1 tablespoon olive oil in a saucepan and cook 2 sliced leeks and 2 grated zucchini (courgettes) for 5–6 minutes, so the vegetables are silky soft. Add 2–3 large handfuls of chopped cavolo nero or silverbeet (swiss chard) and cook for another 2–3 minutes, until the greens are wilted and dark green. Put in a bowl with 500 g (1 lb 2 oz/2 cups) fresh ricotta, season well and toss through your favourite pasta.

soft tofu is also used in a recipe on page...
135.

soft tofu

grandma's tofu and pork hotpot

Place a 300 g (10¹/₂ oz) block of soft (silken) tofu on some paper towel to drain any excess liquid. Cut into 2 cm (³/₄ inch) cubes and place on several layers of paper towel. Heat a good splash of vegetable oil in a heavy-based casserole dish and cook 2 chopped garlic cloves and 2 teaspoons grated ginger for a few seconds so they just flavour the oil but don't burn. Add 300 g (10¹/₂ oz) minced (ground) pork and stir-fry for 3–4 minutes, so the pork is no longer pink. Quickly combine 500 ml (17 fl oz/2 cups) chicken stock, 2 tablespoons oyster sauce, 2 teaspoons cornflour (cornstarch) and a pinch of sugar and salt in a bowl and pour into the pan. Bring to the boil, so it thickens a little and add 80 g (2³/₄ oz/¹/₂ cup) peas. Place on a lid and cook on a low heat for 2–3 minutes. Add the tofu and gently stir through, being careful not to break up the tofu. Serve with a sprinkling of white pepper.

silky fried tofu with chilli pepper and lemon

Place a 600 g (1 lb 5 oz) block of soft (silken) tofu on some paper towel to drain any excess liquid. Combine 1 teaspoon black pepper, 1 teaspoon chilli flakes and 1 tablespoon sea salt in a bowl. Cut the tofu into 2–3 cm (³/₄–1¹/₄ inch) cubes. Place the pieces on some more paper towel while you heat the oil to fry in. Fill a wok half full of oil and heat over a high heat until the surface shimmers gently. Put 125 g (4¹/₂ oz/1 cup) cornflour (cornstarch) in a bowl. Dip several pieces of tofu at a time in the flour and directly into the hot oil and fry for 1–2 minutes, until nicely golden. Place the cooked tofu on a plate, sprinkle with the seasoning and serve with a scattering of chopped coriander (cilantro) leaves and stems and a generous amount of lemon wedges on the side.

steamed tofu with ginger and spring onion

Place a 600 g (1 lb 5 oz) block of soft (silken) tofu on some paper towel to drain any excess liquid. Cut into 3 cm (1¹/₄ inch) cubes and place in a heatproof bowl. Have a wok of water boiling and a steamer ready to go. Combine 3 tablespoons chicken stock, 1 tablespoon light soy sauce and a good pinch of sugar in a bowl and pour the mixture over the tofu. Place the bowl in the steamer, cover and steam for 10 minutes. Sprinkle 2 teaspoons finely grated ginger and 2 finely sliced spring onions (scallions) over the steamed tofu. Heat 2 tablespoons light cooking oil and 1 teaspoon sesame oil in a saucepan until smoking hot and pour over the tofu so the ginger and spring onions sizzle and flavour the oil.

sour cream is also used in recipes on pages...
15, 23, 55, 61, 63, 65, 99, 141 and 143.

sour cream

three ways with

winter mash with bacon and sour cream

Stir-fry 2 **bacon slices** and 2 finely chopped **onions** in a splash of sizzling **olive oil** for 4–5 minutes. Add 60 g (2¼ oz) **butter** to the saucepan and stir over a gentle heat to melt the butter. Set aside. Cook 4 peeled and quartered **large potatoes** in a saucepan of boiling water for 20 minutes. Drain and return the potatoes to the hot pan with 125 g (4½ oz/½ cup) **sour cream** or **crème fraîche**. Mash for a few minutes then beat with a wooden spoon to really soften and cream the potatoes. Quickly reheat the onion mixture and stir through the potatoes. Taste for seasoning and serve with winter **meat dishes**.

creamy scrambled eggs with dill

Beat 6 **eggs** with 3 tablespoons **sour cream** or **crème fraîche**, a small handful of roughly chopped **dill** and a pinch of **salt**. Heat 40 g (1½ oz) **butter** in a non-stick frying pan. When the butter is gently sizzling, pour in the egg mixture. Let it cook in the pan without stirring for a minute. When the edges start to puff up, gently fold the eggs towards the centre of the pan. Repeat until the eggs are firm to your liking. Remove from the heat and keep in the warm pan while you toast and butter your **bread**. Serves 2 with **smoked salmon**.

chicken and bacon goulash

Cook 2 chopped **bacon slices** and 1 chopped **onion** in a splash of hot **oil** for 4–5 minutes, so both the bacon and onion sizzle in the hot pan. Add 2 thinly sliced **boneless, skinless chicken breasts** and stir-fry for 5 minutes, to lightly brown the chicken. Add 125 ml (4 fl oz/ ½ cup) **white wine** to the hot pan so it sizzles. Cook until the wine has almost evaporated and stir through 250 g (9 oz/1 cup) **sour cream** or **crème fraîche**, 2 tablespoons **sun-dried tomato paste (concentrated purée)** and simmer for 5 minutes. Remove from the heat and stir through a handful of chopped **flat-leaf (Italian) parsley**. Serve with **potato mash**, **risoni** or **rice**.

white wine is also used in recipes on pages...
53 and 123.

white wine

chicken cacciatore

Heat a few splashes of **light olive oil** in a large heavy-based casserole dish. Cook **4 chicken forequarters** in the sizzling oil for 5–6 minutes, turning the pieces often, so they are well browned, then remove. Cook 1 chopped **onion**, 2 chopped **garlic cloves**, 1 chopped **carrot** and 1 sliced **celery stalk** in the dish for 2–3 minutes, to soften the vegetables. Add 250 ml (9 fl oz/ 1 cup) **white wine** to the pan and let it sizzle for a few minutes until almost evaporated. Return the chicken to the dish with 400 g (14 oz) tinned **chopped tomatoes**, 90 g (3¼ oz/½ cup) **black olives** and 250 ml (9 fl oz/1 cup) water. Season well, cover and simmer for 50 minutes. Stir through a handful of chopped **flat-leaf (Italian) parsley** and serve with **potato mash** or **soft polenta**.

tipsy lemon risotto

Heat 500 ml (17 fl oz/2 cups) **white wine** and 500 ml (17 fl oz/ 2 cups) **chicken stock** in a saucepan so it simmers gently. Cook 1 chopped **onion** and 2 chopped **garlic cloves** in 40 g (1½ oz) sizzling **butter** until they are softened. Add 330 g (11¾ oz/1½ cups) **risotto rice** and stir-fry for a minute to evenly coat the rice and so it looks shiny. Add 125 ml (4 fl oz/½ cup) of the hot stock to the pan and stir constantly until it has almost all been absorbed. Repeat this process until all the stock is in with the rice and keep stirring until the rice is soft but still has a little bit of a bite to it. Stir in 40 g (1½ oz) **butter**, 50 g (1¾ oz/½ cup) finely grated **parmesan**, a really good squeeze of **lemon juice** and **salt** and **black pepper**. Serve with little more grated **parmesan** on top.

vanilla peaches

Bring 500 ml (17 fl oz/2 cups) **white wine** to the boil and add 220 g (7¾ oz/1 cup) **sugar** and 1 **vanilla bean**, split down the middle so all those tasty, tiny seeds flavour the sweet syrup. Add 4 **small peaches** or 8 **apricots** and simmer for 10 minutes so they are really soft. Put the fruit on a plate and boil the poaching liquid until it has reduced by half then pour over the fruit. Allow the fruit to cool in the syrup. Mix together 125 g (4½ oz/½ cup) **light sour cream** or **crème fraiche** and 1 tablespoon **soft brown sugar** and serve with the peaches.

white wine / fridge

yoghurt is also used in recipes on pages...
67, 87, 123, 139, 147 and 201.

yoghurt

turkish cucumber salad

Combine 250 g (9 oz/1 cup) plain yoghurt, 1 teaspoon ground cumin, 1 crushed garlic clove, 1 tablespoon white vinegar and 1 teaspoon sea salt in a bowl. Chop 4 Lebanese (short) cucumbers into 2 cm (3/4 inch) pieces and combine in a large bowl with 2 large handfuls mint. Spoon the yoghurt dressing over the top and serve straight up.

cauliflower in spiced yoghurt

Cook 500 g (1 lb 2 oz/4 cups) cauliflower florets in boiling water for 5 minutes and drain well. Stir-fry 1 chopped onion, 1 chopped garlic clove, 2 teaspoons chopped ginger, 1/2 teaspoon ground ginger and 2 sliced green chillies in a splash of vegetable oil for 5 minutes on a gentle heat. Add the cauliflower pieces and cook for 10 minutes, so the cauliflower slowly begins to turn golden and softens. Add 250 g (9 oz/1 cup) Greek-style yoghurt to the pan and cook over a gentle heat to warm through. Stir through 1/2 teaspoon garam masala and serve with basmati rice and warm naan bread.

smoky eggplant, cumin and mint dip

Prick 1 large eggplant (aubergine) all over with a fork and place it and a whole head of garlic on a baking tray and into a really hot oven for 10–15 minutes, until the eggplant looks puffed up and the garlic quite golden. Remove and allow to cool. Peel the eggplant and put the flesh into a food processor. Cut the garlic in half and squeeze out the soft insides into the food processor with 3 tablespoons tahini, 125 g (4 1/2 oz/1/2 cup) plain yoghurt, 1 teaspoon ground cumin, a handful of mint, a good squeeze of a lemon and 3 tablespoons olive oil and blend to a chunky consistency. Season well and serve with some fingers of toasted bread.

3 ways with...
ingredients from
the freezer

berries are also used in recipes on pages...
69, 151 and 163.

berries

three ways with

maple berry compote

Defrost 150 g (5¹/₂ oz/2 cups) frozen **mixed berries** (try your favourite berry or a combination of a few) in a bowl. Add 2 teaspoons **cornflour (cornstarch)** and stir around well to evenly combine. Bring 125 ml (4 fl oz/¹/₂ cup) **maple syrup** to the boil in a saucepan. Add the berry mixture and stir a few times, reduce the heat to low and simmer for 3–4 minutes, so the liquid is thick and syrupy. Remove from the heat, put in a bowl and allow to cool. Serve dolloped over **pikelets**, **hotcakes** or **thick buttered toast**.

messy berry pav

Sit 500 g (1 lb 2 oz) frozen **mixed berries** (or your favourite frozen berry) in a sieve over a bowl to completely defrost. Put the drained berry juice in a saucepan with 3 tablespoons **sugar**, bring to the boil and simmer for a couple of minutes, until thickened slightly, and allow to cool. Crumble 6 **small meringues** into a ceramic dish (about 8 cm/3¹/₄ inches across). Whip up 300 ml (10¹/₂ fl oz) **pouring (whipping) cream** with 1 teaspoon **natural vanilla extract** and 60 g (2¹/₄ oz/¹/₂ cup) **icing (confectioners') sugar** until the whisk leaves soft peaks when it is removed. Spoon the cream over the meringues. Spoon the berries over the cream and drizzle the syrup all over.

blueberry sour cream pudding

Have your oven hot and ready at 180°C (350°F/Gas 4). Grease a 1–1.5 litre (35–52 fl oz/4–6 cup) baking dish with **butter**. Blend 125 g (4¹/₂ oz) very soft **butter** and 185 g (6¹/₂ oz/1 cup) **soft brown sugar** in a food processor for 2 minutes, until smooth. With the motor running, add 1 **egg** and blend for a few seconds. Add 300 g (10¹/₂ oz) **light sour cream** or **crème fraîche** and blend until smoothly combined with the other ingredients. With the motor running, slowly add 125 g (4¹/₂ oz/1 cup) **self-raising flour** until it is all smoothly combined. Put in a bowl and quickly stir through 150 g (5¹/₂ oz/1 cup) frozen **blueberries**. Spoon into the baking dish and put into the oven for 1 hour. It will still be soft in the centre. Serve with **custard** or **vanilla ice cream**.

broad beans are also used in a recipe on page...
21.

broad beans

broad bean, artichoke and marinated feta salad

Cook 310 g (11 oz/2 cups) frozen **broad beans** in boiling water for 5 minutes. Drain, remove the skins and put in a bowl with 3 tablespoons **olive oil** and 1 tablespoon **red wine vinegar**. Add 6 halved **marinated** or **grilled artichokes** and 2–3 handfuls **baby rocket (arugula) leaves**. Toss all around to combine and evenly coat in the dressing. Top with 150 g (5^1/$_2$ oz/1 cup) crumbled **marinated feta** and sprinkle over 2 tablespoons roughly chopped **dill**. This makes a great side to grilled lamb.

creamy broad bean mash

Defrost and peel 310 g (11 oz/ 2 cups) frozen **broad beans**. Cook 1 peeled and roughly chopped **potato** in boiling water for 10 minutes. Add the beans and cook for a further 5 minutes. Drain and return to the warm pan with 40 g (1^1/$_2$ oz) **butter** and 2 tablespoons **milk** and mash until combined but still chunky. Season really well and serve with **grilled lamb**, **tuna steaks** or as part of an antipasto platter.

broad bean and avocado guacamole

Peel 310 g (11 oz/2 cups) frozen **broad beans** and cook in boiling water for 10 minutes. Drain and peel, then put in a food processor with a couple of tablespoons of boiling water and process to a smooth paste. Put in a bowl and add 1 **avocado**, 250 g (9 oz/1 cup) **light sour cream** or **crème fraîche**, 1 chopped **small red onion**, 1 small handful chopped **coriander (cilantro) leaves**, a squeeze of **lime juice** and a dash of **Tabasco**. Mash until combined but still chunky. Season well and enjoy as a dip with warm **bread** or a side to **nachos** or Mexican-flavoured dishes.

corn is also used in a recipe on page... 109.

corn

golden cornbread

Have your oven hot and ready at 200°C (400°F/Gas 6). Combine 125 g (4¹/₂ oz/1 cup) plain (all-purpose) flour, 150 g (5¹/₂ oz/ 1 cup) polenta, 1 tablespoon baking powder with a generous pinch of salt and sugar in a bowl. Make a well in the centre. Combine 250 ml (9 fl oz/1 cup) milk, 250 g (9 oz/1 cup) light sour cream or crème fraîche, 3 eggs and 300 g (10¹/₂ oz/2 cups) frozen corn in a bowl and add to the flour mixture. Stir for a minute, but don't overmix. Heat a generous splash of light olive oil in an ovenproof frying pan or casserole dish and swirl around to coat the bottom of the pan. When smoking hot, pour in the corn batter and cook for 1 minute, letting it sizzle in the pan. Cook in the oven for 25 minutes, or until golden and puffed. Remove and allow to cool for a few minutes before turning out onto a larger plate or chopping board. Cut into wedges or squares to serve.

corn fritters

Put 150 g (5¹/₂ oz/1 cup) defrosted frozen corn in a bowl with 3 chopped spring onions (scallions), 125 g (4¹/₂ oz/¹/₂ cup) sour cream or crème fraîche, 2 eggs, 60 g (2¹/₄ oz/¹/₂ cup) self-raising flour and a good seasoning of salt and black pepper. Stir until evenly combined and the batter is smooth and thickly coats the corn. Heat a splash of vegetable oil in a frying pan. Spoon in 2 tablespoons of the mixture to make a fritter and cook for 2–3 minutes each side, until golden. This mixture makes 8 fritters to enjoy with bacon, eggs and home-style tomato relish.

corn, capsicum and coriander stir-fry

Heat a good splash of vegetable oil in a hot wok and stir-fry 2 chopped garlic cloves and 3 chopped spring onions (scallions) for a few seconds to flavour the oil. Add 1 sliced red capsicum (pepper), stir-fry for 1 minute then add 300 g (10¹/₂ oz/ 2 cups) defrosted frozen corn. Stir-fry for 3–4 minutes then add 2 large handfuls chopped coriander (cilantro) leaves, 2 tablespoons light soy sauce and 1 tablespoon red wine vinegar. Stir, cover with a lid and cook for 2 minutes. Serves 2.

filo

mushroom and feta pie

Have your oven hot and ready at 180°C (350°F/Gas 4). Melt 60 g (2 1/4 oz) **butter** and set aside. Lay 4 sheets of **filo** on top of each other, brushing the melted butter between each sheet. Place the sheets in a 22–25 cm (8 1/2–10 inch) round baking dish or cake tin, letting the long ends overlap. Repeat the process with 4 more sheets of **filo** but lay them in the dish in the opposite direction. Remove the stems from 4 **large flat mushrooms** and cut the caps in quarters. Place the mushroom pieces over the filo and scatter 150 g (5 1/2 oz/1 cup) roughly crumbled **feta** on top. Beat 3 **eggs** in a bowl with 125 ml (4 fl oz/ 1/2 cup) **pouring (whipping) cream** and a good grinding of **black pepper**. Pour over the mushrooms. Fold over the edges of the filo and gently crush to make a rustic border. Brush with any remaining butter and bake for 30 minutes, until the pastry is crisp and golden.

lamb and feta filo parcels

Have your oven hot and ready at 180°C (350°F/Gas 4). Season 4 **lamb leg roasting fillets** (about 185 g/6 1/2 oz each) really well. Heat a splash of **olive oil** in a very hot frying pan and cook the lamb for 4 minutes, turning every minute, until brown all over. Remove and allow to cool. Mash 4 tablespoons **soft feta** (try a marinated feta) with a fork and rub over the lamb. Place 1 sheet of **filo** on top of another and place 1 piece of lamb running along the short end. Brush the edges with a little melted butter. Fold along the length, folding in the sides as you go, to make a neat parcel. Repeat to make 4. Place on a tray and bake for 25 minutes, until golden. Serve with a simple **tomato, red onion and mint salad**.

salmon dill pie

Have your oven hot and ready at 180°C (350°F/Gas 4). Melt 60 g (2 1/4 oz) **butter**. Lay 4 sheets of **filo** on a flat surface, brushing between each layer with the butter. Put 400 g (14 oz) tinned, drained **red salmon** in a bowl and roughly mash. Add 250 g (9 oz/ 1 cup) **Greek-style yoghurt**, 1 tablespoon finely chopped **dill**, 2 **eggs**, 75 g (2 3/4 oz/1/2 cup) crumbled **feta** and a good squeeze of **lemon juice**, and season well. Spoon the mixture to fit into a small ovenproof dish. Carefully place the filo on top, fold over the edges and gently crush up, to give a rustic effect, and bake for 25–30 minutes, until golden.

ice cream is also used in a recipe on page...
157.

ice cream

tutti-frutti ice cream

Soften 1 litre (35 fl oz/4 cups) vanilla ice cream. Blend 315 g (11 oz/1 cup) roughly chopped mango flesh with 2 tablespoons icing (confectioners') sugar in a food processor until smooth. Add to the ice cream along with 3 tablespoons passionfruit pulp, stirring quickly to combine. Spoon into a freezer container and into the freezer until firm.

adults only affogato

Place 2 scoops of vanilla ice cream each into 4 glasses and keep in the freezer until needed. To serve, make 250 ml (9 fl oz/ 1 cup) hot strong coffee. Pour 1 tablespoon of liqueur over each serve of the ice cream (try grappa, Frangelico or Grand Marnier), top with a quarter of the coffee for each serve and enjoy.

strawberry meringue parfait

Soften 1 litre (35 fl oz/4 cups) vanilla ice cream in a large bowl. Put 250 g (9 oz/1²/₃ cups) hulled strawberries and 1 tablespoon icing (confectioners') sugar in a food processor and blend until the strawberries are finely chopped, then add to the ice cream. Roughly break up meringues to give about 2 cups in volume and put in the ice cream bowl. Stir to evenly combine the ingredients. Spoon into a loaf (bar) tin and freeze. When firm, remove from the tin and cut into thick slices.

peas are also used in recipes on pages...
15, 51, 115, 119, 137 and 147.

peas

pea curry

Cook 1 chopped **onion**,
1 teaspoon grated **ginger** and
1 chopped **large red chilli** in a
splash of **vegetable oil** until the
onion softens and gently sizzles
in the oil. Add 2 tablespoons **mild
curry powder** and cook for a
minute, to release the hidden
spices in the powder. Add
3 chopped **tomatoes** and 250 ml
(9 fl oz/1 cup) water and bring to
the boil. Add 155 g (5½ oz/1 cup)
frozen **peas**, return to the boil and
reduce the heat to a rapid simmer
for 15 minutes, so the sauce has
thickened. Stir through 20 g
(¾ oz) **butter**, taste for seasoning
and serve with **rice**.

rigatoni with pea, eggplant and mint sauce

Cook 400 g (14 oz) **rigatoni** in
boiling water for 8–10 minutes.
Drain and return to the warm pan.
Meanwhile, heat 3 tablespoons
olive oil in a frying pan over a high
heat and, when smoking hot, add
1 finely cubed **eggplant (aubergine)**
and cook for 3–4 minutes, until
golden. Add 1 chopped **garlic
clove**, 1 teaspoon **dried mint** and
cook for 1 minute. Add 500 ml
(17 fl oz/2 cups) **tomato passata
(puréed tomatoes)** and 155 g
(5½ oz/1 cup) defrosted frozen
peas and cook for 4–5 minutes.
Serve over or tossed through the
pasta with **parmesan** or a dollop
of **fresh ricotta**.

pea soup with crispy prosciutto and ricotta toasts

Cook 1 chopped **onion** in 40 g
(1½ oz) of sizzling **butter** for
2–3 minutes. Add 465 g (1 lb/
3 cups) frozen **peas** and 1 litre
(35 fl oz/4 cups) **chicken stock**
and boil for 10 minutes. Pour into
a food processor and blend for
1 minute, until smooth, and return
to the clean saucepan. Taste for
seasoning and leave on a low heat.
Heat a splash of **olive oil** in a
frying pan and cook 4–6 slices
of **prosciutto** in the hot oil for
2 minutes each side, so they
brown and crisp. Remove from the
pan. Toast 4 slices of **sourdough**
until golden, and thickly spread
3 tablespoons **ricotta** on each slice.
Crumble the prosciutto over the
soup and serve with the toasts.

pizza bases are also used in recipes on pages...
21 and 37.

pizza bases

bruschetta pizza with tomato, anchovy and basil

Have your oven hot and ready at 220°C (425°F/Gas 7) and place a baking tray in the oven. Mix together 2 crushed **garlic cloves** and 3 tablespoons **olive oil** and brush over 2 frozen **pizza bases**. Cook the pizzas in the oven for 12–15 minutes, until golden, then set aside. Meanwhile, put 3 roughly chopped ripe and tasty **large tomatoes**, 6–8 chopped **anchovy fillets**, 2 crushed **garlic cloves** and 2–3 tablespoons **olive oil** in a non-stick frying pan. Stir over a low heat for 2–3 minutes, until just warm, to bring out the flavours of the ingredients. Put in a bowl and toss through 1 large handful roughly torn **basil**, season well with **salt** and **black pepper** and arrange over the warm pizza bases.

spicy spanish pizza

Have your oven hot and ready at 220°C (425°F/Gas 7) and place a baking tray in the oven. Spread 1 tablespoon **tomato paste (concentrated purée)** over a **pizza base**. Top with 8 thin slices of **spicy Spanish salami**, 2 roughly chopped **marinated eggplant (aubergine)** slices and 4 sliced **marinated artichokes** (both available from a delicatessen) and 100 g (3 1/2 oz) finely sliced **manchego cheese**. Place on the hot tray and into the oven for 15 minutes.

potato, onion and rosemary pizza

Have your oven hot and ready at 220°C (425°F/Gas 7) and place a baking tray in the oven. Brush a large **pizza base** (about 25 cm/ 10 inches across) with **olive oil** and 1 crushed **galic clove**. Cover the entire base with 1 very thinly sliced **all-purpose potato** (desiree is best). Top with 1 thinly sliced **onion**, 1 teaspoon **rosemary needles** and 1 teaspoon **sea salt** and **black pepper**. Drizzle a little more **oil** over and cook for 20–25 minutes, until the edges of the pizza and the onion are golden and crispy.

prawns are also used in recipes on pages...
25, 31, 115, 117, 121, 135, 147, 197, 199 and 215.

prawns

cheat's tom yum soup

Boil 500 ml (17 fl oz/2 cups) water and add 2–3 tablespoons **tom yum paste**. Stir around for 1 minute then add 1 chopped firm **tomato**, 8–10 peeled and deveined **raw prawns (shrimp)**, 4–6 torn **makrut (kaffir lime) leaves**, a large handful of your favourite **mushrooms**, sliced, a handful of halved **baby corn** and 1 tablespoon each **lime juice** and **fish sauce**. Simmer for 5 minutes, until the prawns are pink and curled and serve hot, topped with a handful of **bean sprouts** and extra **fish sauce** on the side.

spicy thai prawns with beans and basil

Top, tail and halve 3 handfuls **green beans** and defrost 500 g (1 lb 2 oz) frozen peeled and deveined **raw prawns (shrimp)**. Heat 125 ml (4 fl oz/¹/₂ cup) **vegetable oil** in a frying pan and, when the surface shimmers, add the beans and sizzle in the hot oil for 5 minutes, so they really soften and start to brown. Place on a plate and drain all but a little oil from the pan. Add 2 tablespoons **red curry paste** and stir-fry for 2–3 minutes, until really fragrant. Add the prawns to the pan and cook for 2 minutes each side, so they become pink and curled. Return the beans to the pan with 125 ml (4 fl oz/¹/₂ cup) **chicken stock**, 1 tablespoon **fish sauce** and a good pinch of **sugar**. Cook until almost all the liquid has gone and stir through 1 large handful sweet, liquoricey **Thai basil** to serve.

chilli prawn linguine

Defrost 16–20 peeled and deveined **raw large prawns (shrimp)**. Cook 400 g (14 oz) **linguine** in boiling water for 8–10 minutes. Drain and return to the warm pan. Meanwhile, heat 3 tablespoons **olive oil** in a large frying pan and cook the prawns for 2 minutes each side so they sizzle, become pink and curl in the oil. Add 3 **garlic cloves** and 2 seeded and chopped **small red chillies** to the pan, stirring around so they soften and flavour the oil. Add a generous squeeze of **lemon juice**, 1 large handful roughly chopped **flat-leaf (Italian) parsley** and a generous seasoning of **salt** and **black pepper**. Add the pasta and cook over a gentle heat for 2–3 minutes.

puff pastry is also used in recipes on pages...

13, 15, 27, 89, 105, 161 and 213.

puff pastry

lamb wellington

Have your oven hot and ready at 220°C (425°F/Gas 7). Toss 4 **lamb leg roasting fillets** (about 185 g/ 6¹/₂ oz each) in a bowl with a splash of **olive oil**, 1 teaspoon **dried oregano** and season with **black pepper**. Cook the pieces in a really hot frying pan for 4 minutes, turning every minute. Remove and allow to cool. Rub 1 tablespoon **olive tapenade** over each piece of lamb and wrap each piece snugly and neatly in a defrosted 12 x 24 cm (4¹/₂ x 9¹/₂ inch) piece of **puff pastry** (half a standard sheet). Brush with **egg yolk** and cut several slits in the top for steam to escape. Place on a lightly oiled baking tray and bake for 25 minutes, until puffed and golden.

puff pastry with tomato, haloumi and mint salad

Have your oven hot and ready at 220°C (425°F/Gas 7). Fold over the edges of a sheet of **puff pastry** to make a 5 mm (¹/₄ inch) border, pressing down with a fork. Bake in the oven for 15 minutes, until puffed and golden. Cover the top of the pastry with 2 thinly sliced **tomatoes** brushed with a little **olive oil**, season well and return to the oven for 5 minutes. Place the tart on a serving plate and top with a handful of **baby rocket (arugula) leaves**, a handful of **mint** and a drizzle of **olive oil**. Heat a splash of **olive oil** in a hot non-stick frying pan and cook 6 thick slices of **haloumi** for 1 minute each side, until golden. Place the grilled haloumi slices over the tart, season with **black pepper** and serve with wedges of **lemon** to squeeze over.

hot apple danish

Have your oven hot and ready at 220°C (425°F/Gas 7). Cut a piece of **puff pastry** into 4 squares and fold over the edges to make a 5 mm (¹/₄ inch) border. Place on a baking tray lined with baking paper. Peel and core 2 **apples** and cut each into 8 wedges. Cook the wedges in a frying pan with 20 g (³/₄ oz) sizzling **butter**, 2 tablespoons **caster (superfine) sugar** and ¹/₂ teaspoon **natural vanilla extract** for 4–5 minutes, turning often so the apples start to soften. Place the apple wedges on the pastry and cook for 20 minutes, so the pastry is puffed and golden. Serve hot with **custard** and **vanilla ice cream**.

Pampas® **5** ready rolled sheets shortcrust pastry

Pampas® **5** ready rolled sheets shortcrust pastry

shortcrust pastry

savoury lamb pie

Have your oven hot and ready at 180°C (350°F/Gas 4). Cook 1 chopped **onion** in a splash of **light olive oil** for a few minutes, sizzling gently in the oil to soften. Add 500 g (1 lb 2 oz) **minced (ground) lamb** and stir-fry over a high heat for 5 minutes so the lamb browns. Add 155 g (5¹/₂ oz/ 1 cup) **peas**, 2 **carrots**, 1 teaspoon **dried oregano**, 500 ml (17 fl oz/ 2 cups) **beef stock** mixed with 1 tablespoon **cornflour (cornstarch)** and 2 tablespoons **worcestershire sauce**. Bring the mixture to the boil for a few minutes, until the sauce thickens. Pour into a baking dish. Top with a sheet of **shortcrust pastry**, trim to fit and press firmly around the edges. Brush with an **egg yolk** mixed with a splash of cold water and bake for 30 minutes, until the pastry is golden.

provençal tomato and cheese tart

Have your oven hot and ready at 180°C (350°F/Gas 4). Defrost a sheet of **shortcrust pastry** and place on a lightly oiled baking sheet. Press around the edges with a fork to mark a border and bake for 10 minutes and allow to cool. Lay thin slices of **gruyère** or **edam** over the entire tart, top with 2 thinly sliced ripe **tomatoes**, ¹/₂ teaspoon **dried basil**, 2 tablespoons grated **parmesan** and a good seasoning of **salt** and **black pepper**. Dot 40 g (1¹/₂ oz) **butter** on top and bake for 20–25 minutes.

asparagus and goat's cheese tart

Have your oven hot and ready at 180°C (350°F/Gas 4). Cut a sheet of frozen **shortcrust pastry** in half and place on a lightly oiled baking tray. Fold over the edges just a little to make a thin border and bake for 15 minutes. Remove and cool. Cut 2 bunches of **thin asparagus** into 10 cm (4 inch) long stalks. Put in a frying pan with 40 g (1¹/₂ oz) **butter**, season well and toss around over a high heat in the sizzling butter for 3–4 minutes. Crumble 3 tablespoons **goat's cheese** over the base of each tart, top with the asparagus and 4 tablespoons grated **parmesan**. Bake for 20 minutes. Serves 2.

spinach is also used in a recipe on page...
39.

spinach

shell pasta with ricotta and spinach

Have your oven hot and ready at 180°C (350°F/Gas 4). Cook 400 g (14 oz) **small shell pasta** in boiling water for 8–10 minutes, drain and return to the warm pot. Meanwhile, put 200 g (7 oz) defrosted frozen **spinach** in a large bowl with 750 g (1 lb 10 oz/3 cups) **ricotta**, 100 g (3½ oz/1 cup) grated **parmesan** and a generous seasoning of **salt** and **black pepper**. Stir to combine and add to the pot with the pasta, stirring well to combine. Spoon into a 3 litre (104 fl oz/12 cup) greased baking dish, top with some extra grated **parmesan** and bake for 30 minutes.

spinach and chickpea curry

Cook 1 chopped **red onion** and 2 chopped **garlic cloves** in a splash of **vegetable oil** for 5 minutes, so the onion gently sizzles and softens. Add 1–2 tablespoons of your favourite **curry powder** or **mild Indian curry paste** and cook for 2 minutes, stir-frying the paste to bring out the spices. Add 400 g (14 oz) tinned **chickpeas**, drained and rinsed, 400 g (14 oz) tinned **chopped tomatoes**, 4–6 finely chopped **sun-dried tomatoes** and 250 ml (9 fl oz/1 cup) water and boil for 10 minutes. Add 200 g (7 oz) defrosted frozen **spinach** and gently simmer for 5 minutes. Serve with **basmati rice** and **yoghurt** on the side.

creamy spinach and leek soup

Cook 2 sliced **leeks** in 40 g (1½ oz) gently sizzling **butter** for 5 minutes so the leeks become soft and silky. Add 2 peeled and chopped **large potatoes** and 750 ml (26 fl oz/3 cups) **chicken stock** and boil for 10 minutes. Add 200 g (7 oz) defrosted frozen **spinach** and cook for a further 5 minutes. Put the mixture in a food processor and blend until smooth. Return to the saucepan, stir through 250 ml (9 fl oz/1 cup) **pouring (whipping) cream** and cook on a gentle heat for 5 minutes.

vine leaves

three ways with

barbecued haloumi in vine leaves

Wrap a 1 cm (1/2 inch) thick slice of **haloumi** firmly in **vine leaves**, leaving a little bit of haloumi sticking out either side of the parcel. Cook each parcel on a really hot barbecue hotplate or in a non-stick frying pan with a splash of **fruity olive oil** until the vine leaves go dark green and crispy and sizzle in the oil. Arrange on a platter with a good squeeze of **lemon juice** and enjoy as a starter.

steamed vine leaf fish with dill and lemon

Place several overlapping **vine leaves** on a chopping board to make a 20 cm (8 inch) square. Place a **white fish fillet** (about 180–200 g/ 6¹/₂–7 oz), skin side down, in the centre of the leaves. Spread 20 g (³/₄ oz) **butter** over the top of the fish, place 2 thin slices of **lemon** on the butter with a sprig of **dill** on the lemon. Season well with **sea salt** and **black pepper** and firmly fold up the edges of the vine leaves to tightly seal. Repeat to make 4 parcels. Place the parcels in a large bamboo steamer and cover with the lid. Place the steamer over a wok or large saucepan of boiling water and steam for 15 minutes.

baked mushrooms and goat's cheese in vine leaves

Drizzle some **fruity olive oil** over the bottom of a small baking tray. Lay 4 **vine leaves** on the base of the tray, so they overlap a little. Remove the stems from 4 **large field mushrooms** and sit them on the vine leaves with 1 tablespoon **soft goat's cheese** in the cap of each mushroom. Drizzle with **olive oil** and a good squeeze of **lemon juice** and top with some freshly ground **black pepper**. Place 4 **vine leaves** on top and bake in a hot oven for 20 minutes. Serve as a starter.

3 ways with...
ingredients from the pantry

almonds are also used in recipes on pages...
35, 41, 117, 123 and 151.

almonds

stir-fried chicken with almonds

Cut 6 **chicken thigh fillets** into quarters and toss around in a bowl with 1 tablespoon **cornflour (cornstarch)**, 2 tablespoons **rice wine** (or white wine) and 2 teaspoons **soy sauce**. Set aside for 10 minutes. Heat 3 tablespoons **vegetable oil** in a wok and, when smoking hot, add half of the chicken and stir-fry for 3–4 minutes then remove to a plate. Repeat with the remaining chicken. Remove all but 1 tablespoon of the oil from the wok and stir-fry 2 chopped **garlic cloves**, 45 g (1³/4 oz/¹/2 cup) **flaked** or **slivered almonds** and 2 sliced **celery stalks** for 1 minute. Add a splash of **rice wine** so it sizzles. Return the chicken to the wok, stir-fry for a few minutes and serve with some finely sliced **spring onion (scallion)** on top.

almond and parsley pesto

Put 155 g (5¹/2 oz/1 cup) lightly toasted **almonds** in a food processor with 2 large handfuls **flat-leaf (Italian) parsley**, 2 large handfuls **basil** and 2 tablespoons **lemon juice**. Combine until roughly chopped and, with the motor running, add 4 tablespoons **olive oil**. Season with **salt** and **black pepper** and stir through 50 g (1³/4 oz/¹/2 cup) finely grated **parmesan**. Toss through any **pasta**, little **boiled potatoes** or serve as a side to **chargrilled salmon steaks**. You can also add 250 g (9 oz/1 cup) **ricotta** and use for a pasta sauce.

buttery chicken and almond curry

Chop 4 **chicken thigh fillets** into large bite-sized pieces and cook the pieces in a few splashes of sizzling **vegetable oil** for 5–6 minutes. Add 1 chopped **onion** and stir-fry for a few minutes to soften. Add 3 tablespoons **chicken tikka curry paste** and stir-fry for 3–4 minutes, to release all the aromatic spices in the paste. Add 250 g (9 oz/ 1 cup) **plain yoghurt** to the pan, 1 tablespoon at a time, stirring well between each addition. When all the yoghurt is incorporated, stir through 125 ml (4 fl oz/¹/2 cup) **pouring (whipping) cream**, 60 g (2¹/4 oz) **butter** and 55 g (2 oz/ ¹/2 cup) **ground almonds** (saving some to sprinkle on top). Cook over a low heat for a few minutes and serve this rich curry with **basmati rice**.

anchovies are also used in recipes on pages...
35, 43, 73, 103, 105, 149, 183, 191, 197 and 205.

anchovies

olive, tomato and anchovy tart

Have your oven hot and ready at 220°C (425°F/Gas 7). Fold over the edges of a sheet of **puff pastry** to make a 1 cm (1/2 inch) border and place on a tray and into the oven for 10 minutes. Remove and spoon over 3 tablespoons **olive tapenade**, smoothing down, and top with 2 finely sliced **tomatoes** and 4–6 **anchovy fillets** (or to taste, depending how much you like them). Return to the oven for 5–8 minutes so the edges of the pastry are puffed. Remove, scatter with torn **basil** and drizzle with some good **olive oil**. Serves 2.

jansson's temptation

Have your oven hot and ready at 180°C (350°F/Gas 4). Peel and finely slice 3 **large all-purpose potatoes** and 1 **onion**. Place several layers of potatoes and onion slices in a small baking dish with 3–4 **anchovy fillets** between each layer. Heat 125 ml (4 fl oz/ 1/2 cup) **thick (double/heavy) cream**, 125 ml (4 fl oz/1/2 cup) **milk**, 20 g (3/4 oz) **butter** and a good pinch of **white pepper** in a saucepan until it just about boils and pour over the potatoes. Cook in the oven for 1 hour, so the top layer of potatoes are golden and crispy and the underneath potatoes are soft and creamy. Serve this classic Scandinavian dish with **roast pork** or **lamb**.

chilli tomato risoni

Cook 1 chopped **onion**, 1 chopped **garlic clove** and 4 **anchovy fillets** in a splash of **olive oil** so the onion gently sizzles and softens. Add 200 g (7 oz/1 cup) **risoni** and 1 teaspoon **chilli flakes** and stir around for a minute to really coat the risoni in the tasty oil. Add 400 g (14 oz) tinned **chopped tomatoes**, 500 ml (17 fl oz/2 cups) **chicken stock** and bring to the boil. Place on a lid and cook on a really low heat for 20 minutes. Remove from the heat and leave for a further 5 minutes with the lid on. Stir through a handful of chopped **flat-leaf (Italian) parsley**, a good grinding of **black pepper** and 50 g (13/4 oz/1/2 cup) grated **parmesan**. Serve with extra grated **parmesan** on top.

artichokes are also used in recipes on pages...
31, 63, 73 and 99.

artichokes

artichoke pesto

Put 4 tinned **artichokes** in a food processor with 3 tablespoons lightly toasted **pine nuts**, 1 handful **flat-leaf (Italian) parsley**, roughly chopped, 1 **garlic clove**, 3 tablespoons **light olive oil**, a good squeeze of **lemon juice** and process to a smooth paste. Put in a bowl and stir through 3 tablespoons grated **parmesan**. Add a good seasoning of **sea salt** and **black pepper**. Serve as a condiment to **cheese and crackers**, toss through **pasta** or little **boiled potatoes** or use as a sauce for **grilled fish** or **roast chicken**.

creamy artichoke soup

Place 6 tinned **artichokes**, 1 peeled and finely chopped **large potato** and 750 ml (26 fl oz/3 cups) **chicken stock** in a saucepan and boil for 10 minutes. Put the mixture in a blender and process for about 30 seconds, until smooth. Return the soup to the saucepan, stir through 250 ml (9 fl oz/1 cup) **thick (double/heavy) cream**, season well and gently heat for 2–3 minutes. Spread a little **ricotta** or **blue cheese** on **toast** and serve with the artichoke soup.

fusilli with feta, artichoke and cherry tomato sauce

Cook 400 g (14 oz) **fusilli** in boiling water for 8–10 minutes. Meanwhile, heat a splash of **olive oil** in a frying pan over a high heat and add 2 **garlic cloves** and 250 g (9 oz) **cherry tomatoes**. Cook for 3–4 minutes, shaking the pan, until the tomatoes begin to split. Add 350 g (12 oz) sliced **marinated artichokes**, drained of excess oil, and 2 tablespoons of the tasty **oil** from the artichokes to the pan and cook for a further 2 minutes. Stir through 150 g (5½ oz/1 cup) crumbled **marinated feta**, a handful of chopped **flat-leaf (Italian) parsley** and some **black pepper**. Add to the pasta, stir to combine and serve. You can also stir through a couple of handfuls of **rocket (arugula)** or **baby English spinach leaves**.

balsamic vinegar is also used in recipes on pages...
35, 97, 189 and 201.

balsamic vinegar

balsamic glazed t-bone

Toss 4 T-bone steaks in a bowl with 125 ml (4 fl oz/^{1}/$_2$ cup) balsamic vinegar, 2 crushed garlic cloves and 2 tablespoons light soy sauce. Leave to sit in the marinade for 30 minutes, or cover and refrigerate for a few hours if you have the time. Heat a grill plate or barbecue so it is really hot and cook the steak for 5–6 minutes each side or to your liking. Serve with a simple salad of tossed sliced tomatoes, sliced red onion and basil.

spicy sour tofu

Cut a 600 g (1 lb 5 oz) block of firm tofu into 2 cm (^{3}/$_4$ in) cubes and place on several layers of paper towel to absorb excess liquid. Heat 250 ml (9 fl oz/1 cup) vegetable oil in the wok. When the surface shimmers, add half the tofu and fry for 4–5 minutes, until dark golden. Remove and repeat to cook the remaining tofu. Drain all but 1 tablespoon of oil from the wok and stir-fry 2 seeded and finely chopped small red chillies, 2 chopped garlic cloves and 3 chopped spring onions (scallions) for a few seconds. Add 2 tablespoons balsamic vinegar, 2 tablespoons soy sauce, 3 tablespoons chicken stock and ^{1}/$_2$ teaspoon sugar to the wok and boil for 1 minute. Add the tofu and toss for 1 minute to coat in the spicy dark sauce and serve with rice and Chinese greens.

spaghetti with balsamic tomatoes

Cook 400 g (14 oz) spaghetti in boiling water for 8–10 minutes. Meanwhile, heat a few generous splashes of olive oil in a large frying pan over a high heat. Add 4 sliced garlic cloves and cook for 1 minute, so the garlic sizzles. Add 500 g (1 lb 2 oz) cherry tomatoes, 2 tablespoons balsamic vinegar and a sprinkling of sugar to the pan, shaking the pan around to cook the tomatoes for 4–5 minutes so they soften and split open. Sprinkle over 1 teaspoon dried oregano or 2 sprigs of fresh and stir to combine. Add the pasta to the pan with 2 handfuls baby rocket (arugula) leaves and 3 tablespoons grated parmesan, tossing around to combine. Serve with extra parmesan the side.

bean thread noodles

chicken noodle hotpot

Chop 3 **skinless, boneless chicken breasts** into bite-sized pieces and toss them in a bowl with 2 teaspoons grated **ginger**, 2 teaspoons **sesame oil** and 2 tablespoons **light soy sauce**. Put 100 g (3¹/₂ oz) **bean thread noodles** in a bowl, cover with boiling water for 8–10 minutes then drain. Put a quarter of a **Chinese cabbage**, chopped into 3 cm (1¹/₄ inch) pieces, in the bottom of a heavy-based casserole dish. Put the noodles on top and the chicken on top of the noodles. Pour over 750 ml (26 fl oz/3 cups) **chicken stock**, slowly bring to the boil then cover and simmer for 15 minutes. Serve topped with 1 large handful chopped **coriander (cilantro) leaves** and 2 sliced **spring onions (scallions)**.

spicy fish soup

Put 100 g (3¹/₂ oz) **bean thread noodles** in a bowl and cover with boiling water for 8–10 minutes, then drain. Put in the bottom of 2 large soup bowls. Boil 1 litre (35 fl oz/4 cups) **fish** or **vegetable stock** and add 2 tablespoons **tom yum paste**, 400 g (14 oz) tinned **chopped tomatoes**, ¹/₂ teaspoon **turmeric** and 1 tablespoon **fish sauce**. Add 300 g (10¹/₂ oz) cubed **white fish fillets** and simmer for 10 minutes. Stir through a handful of chopped **coriander (cilantro) leaves**, 2 tablespoons **lime juice** and pour over the noodles. Serves 2.

spicy pork noodles

Put 100 g (3¹/₂ oz) **bean thread noodles** in a bowl and cover with boiling water for 8–10 minutes, then drain. Heat 2 tablespoons **vegetable oil** in a hot wok and add 3 chopped **spring onions (scallions)**, 1 teaspoon grated **ginger** and 2 teaspoons **Chinese chilli garlic sauce** and stir-fry for just a few seconds. Add 300 g (10¹/₂ oz) **minced (ground) pork** and stir-fry for 5 minutes. Add 250 ml (9 fl oz/1 cup) **chicken stock**, 1 tablespoon **light soy sauce** and a good pinch of **sugar** and **salt**. Stir to combine then add the noodles, tossing all the ingredients around in the wok. Cook for 7–8 minutes, so the sauce thickens and coats the noodles and pork. Serve hot with some extra sliced **spring onions (scallions)** on top.

buckwheat noodles

buckwheat noodle salad with grilled lamb, mint and feta

Cook 300 g (10½ oz) buckwheat noodles in boiling water for 3 minutes. Rinse and drain really well, shaking out as much excess water as possible. Toss the noodles with 1 tablespoon of the oil from a jar of soft marinated feta. Rub sea salt and black pepper over 2 lamb backstrap or loin fillets (about 300 g/ 10½ oz each) and cook the lamb in a splash of hot vegetable oil for 3–4 minutes each side, so they are still pink in the middle (or 2 minutes each side if using smaller loin fillets). Remove and rest for 5 minutes before finely slicing across the grain. Add the lamb to the noodles with a handful each of roughly chopped mint and flat-leaf (Italian) parsley, 150 g (5½ oz/1 cup) crumbled marinated feta, 1 tablespoon of oil from the feta and 1 tablespoon balsamic vinegar. Gently toss to combine and serve.

japanese mushroom and leek broth

Cook 200 g (7 oz) buckwheat noodles in boiling water for 2–3 minutes and drain. Heat a splash of vegetable oil and a drizzle of sesame oil in a saucepan and stir-fry 1 sliced leek for 3–4 minutes. Add 2 handfuls each trimmed shiitake, enoki and oyster mushrooms, and stir-fry to soften for a few minutes. Add 750 ml (26 fl oz/3 cups) chicken or vegetable stock, 2 tablespoons light soy sauce and a ½ teaspoon sugar. Simmer for 5 minutes. Put the noodles in bowls and ladle over the broth.

buckwheat noodles with smoked chicken, lime and sesame

Cook 300 g (10½ oz) buckwheat noodles in boiling water for 3 minutes. Rinse and drain really well, shaking out as much excess water as possible, and place into a bowl with 2 shredded smoked chicken breasts, 3–4 finely sliced spring onions (scallions), 1 finely sliced Lebanese (short) cucumber and 2–3 handfuls frisée. Combine 1 tablespoon each light soy sauce, black Chinese or balsamic vinegar, lime juice, sesame oil and ½ teaspoon sugar in a bowl and stir until the sugar has dissolved. Pour over the salad ingredients, toss well to evenly coat the noodle salad in the dressing and serve sprinkled with a tablespoon of toasted sesame seeds.

tortillas are also used in a recipe on page...
45.

burritos and tortillas

chilli bean burrito

Cook 1 chopped **onion** and
2 chopped **garlic cloves** in a frying
pan with a splash of sizzling **olive
oil** for 3–4 minutes, to soften the
onion. Add 1 teaspoon each **dried
oregano**, **ground cumin** and **chilli
flakes**, and stir for 1 minute. Add
500 g (1 lb 2 oz) **minced (ground)
beef** or **pork** and stir-fry for
8–10 minutes, to evenly brown.
Add 400 g (14 oz) tinned **kidney
beans** (drained, not rinsed, and
roughly mashed), 400 g (14 oz)
tinned **chopped tomatoes**, 125 ml
(4 fl oz/^{1}/$_2$ cup) water and a good
seasoning of **salt** and **black
pepper**. Boil the mixture then
rapidly simmer for 15 minutes,
stirring often. Meanwhile, wrap
4–6 **burritos** in foil and warm in
a 180°C (350°F/Gas 4) oven for
10 minutes. Serve the chilli beef
wrapped in the warm burritos with
some **sour cream** or **guacamole**
on the side.

artichoke, salami and olive tortilla

Have your oven hot and ready at
220°C (425°F/Gas 7). Place a large
tortilla on a baking tray. Spread
2 tablespoons **olive tapenade** over
the tortilla and top with 3 sliced
and drained **marinated artichokes**,
6–8 thin slices of **salami**, 1 sliced
tomato,150 g (5^1/$_2$ oz/1 cup)
grated **mozzarella** and a good
grinding of **black pepper**. Place
another **tortilla** on top and cook in
the oven for 5 minutes. Turn over
and cook for a further 5 minutes,
or until golden. Cut each tortilla into
6–8 wedges and serve as a snack.

roasted vegetable, feta and mint quesadilla

Spread a couple of pieces of
grilled eggplant (aubergine) and
red capsicum (pepper) (both
available from the delicatessen
section at the supermarket)
over a **burrito**. Crumble over 75 g
(2^3/$_4$ oz/^{1}/$_2$ cup) **feta**, 75 g (2^3/$_4$ oz/
^{1}/$_2$ cup) grated **mozzarella** and
a handful of roughly torn **mint**.
Sprinkle over ^{1}/$_2$ teaspoon **chilli
flakes** and place another **burrito**
on top. Have a large non-stick
frying pan hot and almost
smoking. Add the quesadilla and
cook for 2 minutes. Flip over and
cook for a couple more minutes.
Remove to a chopping board and
cut into wedges. Serves 2.

butterbeans

tapas butterbeans

Cut 3 ripe and tasty **tomatoes** in half and squeeze the juice and seeds into a bowl. Chop the tomatoes into bite-sized chunks. Heat 3 tablespoons **olive oil** in a frying pan and stir-fry the tomato pieces with 2 **garlic cloves** over a high heat for a few minutes to soften. Add 400 g (14 oz) tinned **butterbeans (lima beans)**, rinsed and drained, 2 teaspoons **tomato paste (concentrated purée)** and a small handful of torn **basil**. Season really well (both the beans and tomato like **salt** and **pepper**). Add the tomato juice and seeds to the pan and cook over a low heat for 5 minutes. Serve with some warm crunchy fresh **bread** as a shared starter.

creamy, garlicky bean dip

Put 400 g (14 oz) tinned **butterbeans (lima beans)**, rinsed and drained, in a saucepan with 3 tablespoons **pouring (whipping) cream**, 20 g (3/4 oz) **butter** and 2 **garlic cloves**, and cook over a gentle heat for 5 minutes (don't let the mixture boil). Put the mixture in food processor and blend until smooth, thick and creamy. Add a splash of **milk** if too thick. Season well with **sea salt** and **black pepper**. Serve with fingers of toasted **Turkish (pide/flat) bread**.

tuscan butterbeans

Heat 2 tablespoons good **fruity olive oil** and 20 g (3/4 oz) **butter** in a saucepan. When the butter starts to sizzle, add 2 chopped **garlic cloves** and 1 **bay leaf** and cook over a gentle heat for 2–3 minutes, to soften the garlic and flavour the oil. Add 400 g (14 oz) tinned **butterbeans (lima beans)**, rinsed and drained, a small handful of roughly chopped **black olives**, a handful of roughly chopped **flat-leaf (Italian) parsley** and a good grinding of **black pepper** to the pan. Cook for 5 minutes over a gentle heat and serve with **grilled lamb cutlets** or **fish**.

cannellini beans are also used in recipes on pages...
17 and 25.

cannellini beans

really chunky white bean and pancetta soup

Cook 1 chopped **carrot**, 1 chopped **onion**, 1 chopped **celery stalk** and 40 g (1½ oz) chopped **pancetta** in a splash of **olive oil** for 2–3 minutes, until the vegetables are a little softened. Add 400 g (14 oz) tinned **cannellini beans**, rinsed and drained, 400 g (14 oz) tinned **chopped tomatoes**, 2 peeled and diced **potatoes** and 1.5 litres (52 fl oz/6 cups) **chicken stock**. Bring to the boil then reduce the heat to simmer for 30 minutes, until the potatoes are cooked through and the soup is really thick. Place a thick slice of **bread** in the bottom of a bowl and spoon over the chunky soup.

white bean and tuna salad

Whisk up 3 tablespoons good **olive oil**, 2 tablespoons **red wine vinegar**, 1 crushed **garlic clove** and 1 teaspoon **dijon mustard** in a bowl. In another bowl, toss together 400 g (14 oz) tinned **cannellini beans**, rinsed and drained, 1 chopped **small red onion**, 1 small handful **black olives**, 2–3 chopped **anchovy fillets**, 1 large handful each roughly chopped **basil** and **flat-leaf (Italian) parsley** and 225 g (8 oz) tinned **tuna** (with a little drizzle of the oil from the tin for extra flavour). Pour over the dressing, gently toss, being careful not to break up the tuna too much, and serve with **warm bread** as a starter.

smoky sausage and bean casserole

Heat a splash of **light olive oil** in a casserole dish and cook 1 chopped **onion** and 2 chopped **smoked Italian sausages** for a few minutes, so the onion softens and sizzles in the oil and the sausage starts to turn crisp around the edges. Add 400 g (14 oz) tinned **cannellini beans**, rinsed and drained, 400 g (14 oz) tinned **tomatoes**, 1 tablespoon **soft brown sugar**, 1 **bay leaf**, a few splashes of **Tabasco** and 125 ml (4 fl oz/½ cup) water. Bring to the boil then reduce the heat to a simmer for 15 minutes. Serve on its own or on toasted **sourdough** or **Turkish (pide/flat) bread**.

capers are also used in recipes on pages...
35, 43, 149, 183 and 187.

capers

upside-down caper and tomato tart

Have your oven hot and ready at 220°C (425°F/Gas 7). Heat 2 tablespoons **olive oil** in an ovenproof frying pan. Add 1 tablespoon **salted small capers** (leave unrinsed as they will season the tart) and 1 teaspoon **rosemary leaves** and stir in the hot oil for 1 minute. Thickly slice 3 very ripe and tasty **tomatoes** and arrange the slices in a single layer on top of the capers and cook for 3–4 minutes, so the tomato softens. Lay a sheet of frozen **puff pastry** on top of the tomatoes, folding in the corners so it fits snugly in the pan. Bake for 15–20 minutes, until the pastry is puffed and golden. Remove and cool for a few minutes before carefully turning over onto a large plate. Add a good grinding of **black pepper** and enjoy with some **baby rocket (arugula) leaves** or a sprinkling of **goat's cheese feta**. Serves 2.

caper and herb sauce

Put 2 slices of **stale bread**, crusts removed, in a food processor with 2 tablespoons rinsed **capers**, 4–6 **anchovy fillets**, 1 teaspoon **dijon mustard**, a handful each of chopped **flat-leaf (Italian) parsley** and **mint** and a good squeeze of **lemon juice**. Blend to a paste and, with the motor running, slowly pour in 125 ml (4 fl oz/^{1}/$_2$ cup) good **olive oil**. Put in a bowl and season well. Use as a side for **grilled salmon**, toss through **green beans** or add to a **potato salad**.

tagliatelle with tuna and lemony capers

Cook 400 g (14 oz) **tagliatelle** or **fettucine** in boiling water for 8–10 minutes. Drain and return to the warm pan. Meanwhile, heat a generous splash of **olive oil** in a frying pan, add 2 tablespoons rinsed **capers** and fry for a few minutes. Add a generous squeeze of **lemon juice**, shake the pan around and put the capers in a bowl. Heat a few more splashes of **oil** in the pan and cook 2 chopped **garlic cloves** over a medium heat and add 3 tablespoons **small black olives** and 375 g (13 oz) tinned **tuna**, drained of oil. Stir for a few minutes to heat the tuna, being careful not to break it up too much. Add a handful of chopped **flat-leaf (Italian) parsley**, toss around gently and serve with the lemony capers on top and a good grinding of **black pepper**.

cashews are also used in a recipe on page...

47.

cashews

three ways with

cashew tabouleh in crisp lettuce

Put 130 g (4³/4 oz/³/4 cup) **burghul (bulgur)** in a dry saucepan and cook over a high heat for 2–3 minutes, shaking the pan constantly. Add 500 ml (17 fl oz/ 2 cups) water and 1 tablespoon **olive oil** to the pan and bring to the boil. Reduce the heat to really low, then place on a tight-fitting lid and cook for 15 minutes. Pour into a bowl and fluff with a fork. Add 2 handfuls **flat-leaf (Italian) parsley**, roughly chopped, 1 small handful **mint**, chopped, 1 finely chopped **Lebanese (short) cucumber** and 155 g (5¹/2 oz/ 1 cup) lightly toasted **cashews**. Whisk up 3 tablespoons each **lemon juice** and **olive oil** and stir well through the salad. Serve in crisp **lettuce cups** as a starter or as a side dish with **lamb**.

cashew and dill pesto

Blend 80 g (2³/4 oz/¹/2 cup) **raw** or **dry-roasted cashews**, 3 tablespoons roughly chopped **dill**, 1 handful **flat-leaf (Italian) parsley**, roughly chopped, 1 **garlic clove**, 3 tablespoons **olive oil** and a good squeeze of **lemon juice** in a food processor to form a rough paste, leaving little pieces of cashew intact. Remove and fold through 3 tablespoons grated **parmesan**. Serve on an antipasto platter, with **roasted pumpkin (winter squash)**, **goat's cheese** or **grilled fish**.

grilled zucchini, cashew and feta salad

Slice 4 **zucchini (courgettes)** into 5 mm (¹/4 inch) strips and chargrill for 3–4 minutes each side. Put in a bowl with 1 small handful **flat-leaf (Italian) parsley**, chopped, 2 tablespoons chopped **dill**, 2 tablespoons **olive oil**, a good squeeze of **lemon juice** and **salt** and **black pepper**. Add 80 g (2³/4 oz/¹/2 cup) **unsalted cashews** to the bowl with 3 handfuls **baby rocket (arugula)** or **baby English spinach leaves**. Toss to combine and arrange on a serving plate. Crumble over 150 g (5¹/2 oz) **soft feta** and serve with some toasted **ciabatta bread**.

chicken stock is also used in recipes on pages...
15, 17, 21, 25, 27, 29, 33, 51, 55, 71, 75, 81, 89, 91, 93, 95, 103, 111, 117, 119, 123, 125, 127, 129, 131, 133, 135, 137, 145, 147, 155, 165, 169, 177, 185, 191, 193, 195, 199 and 211.

chicken stock

chicken noodle soup

Cook 120 g (4¹/4 oz) **angel hair pasta** or **egg vermicelli** in boiling water for 3–4 minutes and drain. Boil 1.5 litres (52 fl oz/6 cups) **chicken stock** and stir through 350 g (12 oz/2 cups) shredded meat and skin of a **barbecued chicken** and 1 large handful chopped **flat-leaf (Italian) parsley**. Add the pasta to the soup and cook for a couple of minutes to heat through. Season well and serve with thickly sliced **buttered toast**.

cajun corn chowder

Fry 1 chopped **onion** and 2 chopped **bacon slices** in 20 g (³/4 oz) sizzling **butter** for 2–3 minutes. Add 400 g (14 oz/ 2 cups) **corn** (defrosted if frozen) 1 teaspoon **Cajun spice mix** and stir-fry for 2 minutes over a high heat. Add 750 ml (26 fl oz/3 cups) **chicken stock**, bring to the boil then simmer for 15 minutes. Blend the mixture in a food processor until smooth then return to the pan with 125 ml (4 fl oz/¹/2 cup) **pouring (whipping) cream** and stir over a gentle heat for 2 minutes to heat through. Serve with a dollop of **sour cream** or **crème fraîche** on top.

cheat's chinese short soup

Bring 1 litre (35 fl oz/4 cups) **chicken stock** to the boil, add 1 tablespoon **light soy sauce** and 1 teaspoon **sesame oil** and simmer while cooking the dumplings. Cook 16 **ready-made Chinese won tons** or **soup dumplings** in boiling water for 2–3 minutes, until they rise to the top. Drain and place the dumplings in the bottom of 4 small soup bowls. Ladle over the hot stock and top each soup with some finely sliced **spring onions (scallions)** and a little extra drizzle of **sesame oil**.

chickpeas are also used in a recipe on page...
81.

chickpeas

chickpea, smoky chorizo and bread salad

Place a **red capsicum (pepper)** in a really hot oven for 10 minutes until puffed up and darkened. Plunge into cold water for a minute then peel and finely slice the flesh and put into a bowl. Cook 2 sliced **chorizos** in a splash of sizzling **olive oil** for 2–3 minutes, so the chorizo sizzles and turns golden. Add the chorizo and any tasty oil from the pan to the capsicums with 400 g (14 oz) tinned **chickpeas**, rinsed and drained, 2 large handfuls **baby rocket (arugula) leaves** and 1 tablespoon **red wine vinegar**. Lightly toast 2 thick slices of **white bread**. Drizzle with a little **olive oil** and season well.

chickpea sesame dip

Blend 400 g (14 oz) tinned **chickpeas**, rinsed and drained, 2 **garlic cloves**, 125 g (4½ oz/ ½ cup) **sour cream** or **crème fraîche**, 2 tablespoons **lemon juice** and 1 teaspoon **sesame oil** in a food processor until really smooth. Add a good amount of **sea salt** and **white pepper** to taste. Serve with a good pinch of **paprika** sprinkled on top and serve as you would with any dip or as a side to **grilled vegetables**.

italian chickpea soup

Heat a few splashes of **olive oil** in a saucepan and cook 1 chopped **onion**, 1 chopped **small fennel bulb**, 1 chopped **carrot**, 1 sliced **celery stalk**, 1 chopped **garlic clove** and 1 teaspoon chopped **rosemary** for 4–5 minutes in the sizzling oil, to soften the vegetables but not brown. Add 400 g (14 oz) tinned **chopped tomatoes**, 400 g (14 oz) tinned **chickpeas**, rinsed and drained, and 750 ml (26 fl oz/ 3 cups) **chicken** or **vegetable stock** and bring to the boil. Simmer for 15 minutes then stir through 3–4 handfuls roughly chopped **English spinach leaves**, and season really well. Simmer for 5 minutes, to wilt the spinach. Serve with warm **foccacia**.

CLAVILEÑO CHOCOLATE A LA TAZA
CLAVILEÑO CHOCOLATE A LA TAZA
CHOCOLATE A LA TAZA

CLAVILEÑO CHOCOLATE A LA TAZA
CLAVILEÑO CHOCOLATE A LA TAZA
CLAVILEÑO CHOCOLATE A LA TAZA
CLAVILEÑO CHOCOLATE A LA TAZA

chocolate is also used in a recipe on page...
157.

chocolate

chocolate pudding

Have your oven hot and ready at 180°C (350°F/Gas 4). Grease a 1 litre (35 fl oz/4 cup) baking dish. Put 200 g (7 oz) dark chocolate and 150 g (5 1/2 oz) butter in a small saucepan over a gentle heat and stir until melted and smooth. Beat 3 eggs and 3 tablespoons caster (superfine) sugar for a minute. Beat in 60 g (2 1/4 oz/ 1/2 cup) self-raising flour until there are no more lumps, then beat in the chocolate mix until smooth and evenly combined. Pour into the prepared dish. Quickly combine 375 ml (13 fl oz/ 1 1/2 cups) boiling water with 3 tablespoons soft brown sugar and 2 tablespoons unsweetened cocoa powder in a jug and carefully pour over the pudding mixture. Bake for 40 minutes. The centre may still be soft and gooey like hot chocolate mousse. Enjoy with vanilla ice cream.

chocolate sauce

Heat 50 g (1 3/4 oz) dark chocolate, 125 ml (4 fl oz/1/2 cup) thick (double/heavy) cream and 1 tablespoon soft brown sugar in a small saucepan over a really gentle heat, stirring all the time until the mixture is totally smooth and all the chocolate has melted. This sauce can be served warm on ice cream, sliced bananas and chopped nuts and will keep well at room temperature for a few hours if made in advance.

over the top chocolate mousse

Put 200 g (7 oz) chopped dark chocolate and 3 tablespoons strong coffee in a bowl over a saucepan of gently simmering water for 8–10 minutes. Remove and beat for a minute, until totally smooth and glossy. Separate 3 eggs and beat the yolks, one at a time, into the chocolate until smooth. Stir through 60 g (2 1/4 oz) melted butter. Beat the egg whites until they are softly peaking then fold into the chocolate mix. Beat 125 ml (4 fl oz/1/2 cup) pouring (whipping) cream to soft peaks, being careful not to overbeat (otherwise the mousse will be grainy). Fold the cream into the mousse, spoon into 4 individual glasses or cups, chill and enjoy.

coconut milk is also used in recipes on pages...
121, 129, 169, 171 and 179.

coconut milk

massaman curry

Cook 1 finely sliced **onion** in a splash of **vegetable oil** for 3–4 minutes. Add 2 tablespoons **soft brown sugar** and 2–3 tablespoons **massaman curry paste** to the pan and cook for 2 minutes. Add 600 ml (21 fl oz) **coconut milk** to the pan and bring to a gentle simmer. Add 2 peeled and quartered **large potatoes** and 3 tablespoons **unsalted raw peanuts** to the pan and cook for 15 minutes. Cut 2 **lamb loin fillets** into small bite-sized pieces and add to the pan, cover and cook for 10 minutes. Stir through 1 tablespoon **fish sauce** and a handful of **basil** and serve with rice. For an ideal garnish, top with some **crisp-fried Asian shallots** and some extra **basil**.

potato and tomato curry

Heat a splash of **oil** in a frying pan and stir-fry 1 sliced **red onion** and 8 unpeeled **baby potatoes** for 4–5 minutes, shaking the pan around so the onions soften and sizzle. Add 2 tablespoons **mild Indian curry paste** (try a balti or madras) and stir-fry for 2–3 minutes, to bring out all the hidden spices in the paste. Add 250 ml (9 fl oz/1 cup) water, bring to the boil and cover with a tight-fitting lid. Cook over a low heat for 15 minutes, stirring often, so the potatoes soften a little. Add 400 ml (14 fl oz) **coconut milk** and 250 g (9 oz) **cherry tomatoes** and bring to a simmer. Cook for 5 minutes, so the tomatoes just begin to split, stir through 1 handful **coriander (cilantro) leaves**, chopped, and serve with some **minted plain yoghurt** and rice.

easy prawn curry

Heat a splash of **vegetable oil** in a pan. Stir-fry 12–16 **raw large prawns (shrimp)**, peeled and deveined, in the sizzling oil for 2–3 minutes, until they curl up and turn pink. Add 1 chopped **onion** and 1 tablespoon **madras curry powder** and stir-fry for 2–3 minutes, to release all the hidden spices in the powder. Add 400 ml (14 fl oz) **coconut milk**, bring to the boil and reduce the heat to simmer for 10 minutes. Add 65 g (2 1/4 oz/ 1/2 cup) **peas** (defrosted if frozen) and 40 g (1 1/2 oz) **butter**, cook over a gentle heat for 2 minutes and serve with **rice**.

coconut milk / pantry

couscous is also used in a recipe on page...

201.

couscous

three ways with

honey pumpkin couscous salad

Have your oven hot and ready at 180°C (350°F/Gas 4). Place 600 g (1 lb 5 oz/4 cups) peeled and chopped bite-sized pieces of pumpkin (winter squash) in a bowl with 1 sliced red onion, 2 tablespoons honey and a good splash of olive oil. Toss around to evenly combine, place on a baking tray and roast for 30 minutes. Meanwhile, place 185 g (6^1/$_2$ oz/ 1 cup) couscous and 20 g (^{3}/$_4$ oz) butter in a bowl. Pour over 250 ml (9 fl oz/1 cup) boiling water and cover tightly for 10 minutes. Fluff once or twice then cover again for 5 minutes. Place the couscous in a bowl and fluff and separate with your fingers. Add the roasted pumpkin mixture to the couscous with 3 tablespoons toasted flaked almonds, toss around and enjoy as a warm salad or as a side to grilled lamb.

smoky spiced couscous

Place 280 g (10 oz/1^1/$_2$ cups) couscous, 1 teaspoon ground cumin and ^{1}/$_2$ teaspoon each ground coriander, chilli powder and paprika in a dry saucepan. Shake the pan over a medium heat for 2–3 minutes, to release the aromas in the spices, being careful not to burn the couscous. Turn the heat off and pour 375 ml (13 fl oz/1^1/$_2$ cups) boiling water into the pan. Add 40 g (1^1/$_2$ oz) butter, stir quickly and cover the pan tightly for 10 minutes. Fluff with a fork and return the lid for 2 minutes. Serve as you would with any couscous; its intense flavour goes really well with simply grilled meats and fish, chargrilled vegetables and yoghurt.

seafood and couscous stew

Heat a splash of olive oil in a frying pan and cook 1 chopped onion and 2 chopped garlic cloves for a few minutes until softened. Add 750 ml (26 fl oz/3 cups) chicken or fish stock, 400 g (14 oz) tinned chopped tomatoes, 3 tablespoons couscous, a generous pinch of saffron and ^{1}/$_2$ teaspoon paprika to the pan and bring to the boil. Simmer for 8–10 minutes then add 400 g (14 oz) white fish fillets, cut into chunks, and 12 peeled and deveined raw prawns (shrimp). Cook over a gentle simmer for 10 minutes, until the fish is white and the prawns are pink and curled. Serve with a handful of flat-leaf (Italian) parsley, roughly chopped, and lemon wedges on the side.

curry powder is also used in recipes on pages...
71, 81, 115 and 177.

curry powder

chicken curry

Have your oven hot and ready at 180°C (350°F/Gas 4). Cut a **whole chicken** into 10–12 pieces. Combine 3 tablespoons **plain (all-purpose) flour** and 3 tablespoons **curry powder** in a bowl and toss the chicken pieces around in the mix to coat all over. Heat a few splashes of **vegetable oil** in a heavy-based casserole dish and cook the chicken in batches for 3–4 minutes, turning often, so they sizzle and turn golden in the oil. Pour off all but 1 tablespoon of oil from the pot and stir 1 chopped **onion** and 2 chopped **garlic cloves** in the spicy oil for 2–3 minutes, so the onion sizzles and turns golden. Return the chicken to the pan with 500 ml (17 fl oz/2 cups) **chicken stock** and 1 chopped **carrot**. Bring to the boil and cook in the oven, uncovered, for 50 minutes. Stir through 130 g (4¾ oz/1 cup) **peas** (defrosted if using frozen) and return to the oven for 10 minutes. Serve with **rice** and warm **naan bread**.

spiced tomato and lentil soup

Cook 1 chopped **onion**, 2 chopped **garlic cloves**, 1 teaspoon chopped **ginger** and 1 tablespoon **mild curry powder** in 40 g (1½ oz) sizzling **butter** for 3–4 minutes, to release all the hidden spices in the powder. Add 125 g (4½ oz/½ cup) **red** or **brown lentils**, 400 g (14 oz) tinned **tomatoes** and 2 litres (70 fl oz/8 cups) water. Bring to the boil and cook on a rapid simmer for 40–45 minutes so the lentils are soft, almost mushy, and you have a thick soup.

curried beef shepherd's pie

Have your oven hot and ready at 180°C (350°F/Gas 4). Cook 4 peeled and chopped **large all-purpose potatoes** in boiling water until soft. Drain and mash until really smooth with 3 tablespoons **milk**. Set aside. Cook 1 chopped **onion** and 1 chopped **carrot** in 40 g (1½ oz) sizzling **butter** for 2–3 minutes. Add 2–3 tablespoons **mild curry powder** and stir-fry for 1 minute, to release all the hidden spices. Add 500 g (1 lb 2 oz) **minced (ground) beef** and stir-fry for 5–6 minutes, to evenly brown, breaking up any large chunks. Add 250 ml (9 fl oz/1 cup) water and boil rapidly for 5 minutes, until almost all the liquid has gone. Stir through 155 g (5½ oz/1 cup) **peas** (defrosted if using frozen). Spoon into a ovenproof dish, top with the potato and cook in the oven for 30 minutes.

curry powder / pantry

desiccated coconut is also used in recipes on pages...
141 and 163.

desiccated coconut

coconut and curry leaf rice

Cook 200 g (7 oz/1 cup) long-grain rice (try basmati) in 1 litre (35 fl oz/4 cups) boiling water for 20 minutes. Drain well. Heat a few splashes of **vegetable oil** in a saucepan and cook 1 sliced **green chilli**, 1 teaspoon **black** or **yellow mustard seeds** and 6–8 **curry leaves** until the mustard seeds start to sizzle and pop. Add 3 tablespoons **desiccated coconut** and stir-fry for 3–4 minutes, until the coconut starts to turn golden. Remove from the heat and stir through the rice and a small handful of chopped **coriander (cilantro) leaves**.

coconut prawns

Peel and devein 12 **raw large prawns (shrimp)**, but leave the tail on for perfect finger food. Put 60 g (2 1/4 oz/1/2 cup) **plain (all-purpose) flour** in a bowl, 2 beaten **eggs** in another small bowl and 90 g (3 1/4 oz/1 cup) **desiccated coconut** in a third bowl. Dip the prawns, one at a time, first in the flour, then the egg and, finally, in the coconut. Press down firmly so the prawns are covered all over with the coconut. Heat a saucepan one-third full of **vegetable oil** over a medium heat until the surface of the oil is shimmering. Cook the prawns in two batches, for 3–4 minutes. Drain on paper towel and serve with your favourite **sweet chilli** or **chilli sauce**.

coconut and makrut leaf chicken curry

Chop 3 **skinless, boneless chicken breasts** into large bite-sized pieces. Put 45 g (1 1/2 oz/1/2 cup) **desiccated coconut** in a saucepan and stir-fry over a medium heat until the coconut turns nicely golden. Remove from the pan. Heat a splash of **vegetable oil** in the saucepan and stir-fry 2 tablespoons **yellow curry paste** in the oil for 2–3 minutes, to release the hidden spices in the paste. Add 4–6 **makrut (kaffir lime) leaves**, 2 teaspoons **soft brown sugar** and the chicken to the pan, stir-frying for 5 minutes, until the chicken is golden all over. Add 400 ml (14 fl oz) **coconut milk** to the pan, bring to the boil then simmer on a low heat for 10 minutes, to gently poach the chicken. Stir through the coconut and serve with **rice**.

dried apricots

three ways with

moroccan chicken with apricots

Chop a **chicken** into 8–10 pieces. Toss the chicken pieces in a bowl with 1 teaspoon **ground cumin**, 1 teaspoon **ground coriander** and a generous seasoning of **salt** and **black pepper**. Heat a few splashes of **light cooking oil** in a large, heavy-based saucepan and cook the chicken pieces in batches for a few minutes each side, until well browned. Return all the chicken to the pan with 180 g (6^1/$_2$ oz/1 cup) **dried apricots**, 6–8 **pitted dates**, 500 ml (17 fl oz/2 cups) **chicken stock** and 3 tablespoons **honey**. Bring to the boil then reduce the heat to low, cover and simmer for 40 minutes, stirring now and then. Stir through 1 large handful **coriander (cilantro) leaves**, roughly chopped, and serve with **couscous**.

smoked chicken, apricot and feta salad

Finely shred 2 **smoked chicken breasts** and put in a bowl with 3 tablespoons chopped **dried apricots**, 1 large handful **flat-leaf (Italian) parsley**, 80 g (2^3/$_4$ oz/ ^{1}/$_2$ cup) toasted **almonds** and 2 large handfuls picked **watercress**. Crumble over 75 g (2^1/$_2$ oz) **marinated feta** (or a mild Danish feta) and gently toss with 2 tablespoons good **olive oil**, 1 tablespoon **red wine vinegar** and a good seasoning of **salt** and **black pepper**.

tipsy apricots with pistachio yoghurt and honey

Put 180 g (6^1/$_2$ oz/1 cup) **dried apricots**, 2 tablespoons **caster (superfine) sugar**, 375 ml (13 fl oz/1^1/$_2$ cups) **water** and 125 ml (4 fl oz/^{1}/$_2$ cup) **white wine** in a saucepan and bring to the boil. Reduce the heat to really low and cover with a tight-fitting lid for 20 minutes. Turn off the heat and allow to sit and soften in the pan until cool. Beat 125 g (4^1/$_2$ oz/ ^{1}/$_2$ cup) **Greek-style yoghurt** with 3 tablespoons chopped **pistachios**. Serve the stewed apricots with the yoghurt and a good drizzling of **honey** all over.

菌朵
自然の風味

NET WT: 100g

菇朵
自然の風味

NET WT: 100g

dried mushrooms are also used in a recipe on page...
165.

dried mushrooms

hot and sour mushroom soup

Soak 6 **dried mushrooms** in 250 ml (9 fl oz/1 cup) boiling water for 15 minutes. Reserve the liquid, remove the stems and slice the caps. Put the mushroom soaking liquid in a saucepan with 1 litre (35 fl oz/4 cups) **chicken stock**, 3 tablespoons **Chinese black vinegar**, 1 tablespoon **light soy sauce**, 1 teaspoon **black pepper**, 140 g (5 oz) tinned and drained **bamboo shoots**, 2 handfuls stemmed and sliced **button mushrooms** and 1 tablespoon **cornflour (cornstarch)**. Gradually bring the soup to the boil, stirring constantly until it thickens slightly. Add the mushrooms and allow to simmer for a few minutes before serving.

simmered mushrooms with tofu

Put 8 **dried mushrooms** in a bowl and cover with boiling water for 20 minutes. Cut off and discard the stems and cut any larger caps in half. Put the caps in a saucepan with 125 ml (4 fl oz/¹/₂ cup) of the soaking liquid, 500 ml (17 fl oz/ 2 cups) water, 2–3 thick slices of **ginger**, 2 tablespoons **light soy sauce**, 2 tablespoons **oyster sauce** and a good pinch of **sugar**. Bring to the boil then reduce the heat and simmer for 15 minutes. Add 185 g (6¹/₂ oz/1 cup) cubed **firm tofu** and cook for a further 5 minutes. Serve with **rice** and **steamed Chinese greens**.

stir-fried mushrooms with chinese cabbage

Put 6–8 **dried mushrooms** in a bowl and cover with boiling water for 20 minutes. Discard the mushroom stems and reserve 2 tablespoons of the soaking liquid. Cut the caps in half. Heat 2 tablespoons **vegetable oil** in a hot wok and stir-fry 1 tablespoon grated **ginger**, 2 chopped **garlic cloves** and 2 chopped **spring onions (scallions)** for a few seconds to flavour the oil. Add the mushrooms and 110 g (3³/₄ oz) tinned **bamboo shoots**, well drained, and stir-fry for 1 minute. Add 135 g (4³/₄ oz/3 cups) sliced **Chinese cabbage** and stir-fry for 2 minutes, until the cabbage has softened, then add the mushroom liquid and 2 tablespoons **light soy sauce** to the wok. Stir-fry for 1 minute and served drizzled with some **sesame oil**.

fish sauce is also used in recipes on pages...
75, 95, 115, 129, 155, 169, 171, 179, 199 and 213.

fish sauce

sweet and sour herbed eggplant salad

Have your oven hot and ready at 220°C (425°F/Gas 7). Combine 2 tablespoons fish sauce, 3 tablespoons lemon juice, 1/4 teaspoon chilli powder and 2 teaspoons sugar in a small bowl and stir to dissolve the sugar. Prick the skin of a large eggplant (aubergine) all over with a fork. Place the eggplant directly onto the middle rack in the oven for 10–15 minutes, so the skin is puffed and burnt. Plunge into cold water for a few minutes. Peel off the skin, tear the flesh into long pieces and place in a bowl with 1 small handful each coriander (cilantro) leaves, mint and basil, and 1 finely sliced red onion. Pour over the dressing and gently toss the ingredients to combine all the flavours.

caramel chicken

Cut 4 chicken leg quarters to separate the legs from the thighs. Heat a splash of vegetable oil in a casserole dish and cook the chicken pieces (you may need to do this in batches) for 3–4 minutes each side so the skin crisps to golden. Drain the oil, then return all the chicken to the pan and add 3 tablespoons fish sauce, 3 tablespoons sugar, 3 crushed garlic cloves, 1/2 teaspoon white pepper, 1 tablespoon dark soy sauce and 500 ml (17 fl oz/2 cups) water, and bring to the boil. Reduce the heat to a gentle simmer for 45–50 minutes, stirring often until almost all the liquid has gone and the sauce thickly coats the chicken.

sweet pork larb in baby cos

Heat 2 tablespoons vegetable oil in a hot wok and stir-fry 3 chopped garlic cloves and 4 finely chopped spring onions (scallions) for 2 minutes, until crisp and golden. Add 3 tablespoons sugar and stir-fry for a minute so it dissolves, then quickly add 250 ml (9 fl oz/ 1 cup) chicken stock (it will sizzle here), 2 tablespoons fish sauce, 1/2 teaspoon chilli powder and 300 g (101/2 oz) minced (ground) pork. Stir-fry over a high heat for 8–10 minutes, until the liquid has almost gone and the pork is quite dark. Spoon the sweet pork into crisp baby cos (romaine) lettuce leaves and serve as a starter with a coriander (cilantro) sprig and lime wedges to squeeze over.

green curry paste

crispy skinned fish in jungle curry

Rub a little **sea salt** and **white pepper** on the skin of 4 **white fish fillets**. Heat a splash of **vegetable oil** in a wok and stir-fry 1 finely chopped **onion** and 2 finely chopped **garlic cloves** for 2 minutes, to soften the onion. Add 2 tablespoons **green curry paste** and a good pinch of **sugar** to the pan and cook for a minute or so, releasing all the hidden spices (that will almost make you want to sneeze). Add 375 ml (13 fl oz/1$\frac{1}{2}$ cups) **chicken stock**, 4–6 **makrut (kaffir lime) leaves** and 1 tablespoon **fish sauce** to the pan and gently simmer while you cook the fish. Heat a few tablespoons of **vegetable oil** in a non-stick frying pan. When smoking hot, add the fish pieces, skin side down, and cook for 3–4 minutes, gently pressing down with a spatula. Turn over and cook for 2–3 minutes. Put into a bowl and spoon over the hot jungle sauce with some extra finely shredded **makrut leaves** on top.

spicy lime and peanut chicken

Whiz-up 3 tablespoons **peanuts** in a food processor until finely chopped. Put in a bowl with 2 tablespoons **green curry paste**, 1 tablespoon **soft brown sugar** and a few splashes of **fish sauce** and **black pepper** for seasoning. Add 4 sliced **chicken thigh fillets**, tossing around to really coat in the spice mix. Heat a good few splashes of **vegetable oil** in a wok or frying pan. When smoking hot, add the chicken and stir-fry for about 8 minutes so the chicken pieces really crisp up. Drain any excess oil from the pan. Add 2 tablespoons **lime juice** and 3 tablespoons **chicken stock** to the pan and stir-fry for a few minutes, until almost all the stock has evaporated. Serve topped with freshly ground **black pepper** and a handful of chopped **coriander (cilantro) leaves**.

green curry with salmon and aromatic herbs

Spoon a few tablespoons of the solidified cream from the top of a 400 ml (14 fl oz) tin of **coconut milk** into a saucepan and boil. When it is really bubbling, add 2 tablespoons **green curry paste** and stir-fry for 2–3 minutes to release all the hidden aromatic spices in the paste. Add 2 teaspoons **sugar** to the pan and cook for a minute then add the remaining coconut milk and 6–8 **makrut (kaffir lime) leaves**. Bring to a gentle simmer then add 400 g (14 oz) bite-sized cubes of **salmon fillet**. Cover with a lid and cook for 5–6 minutes, to gently poach the salmon. Remove from the heat and stir though 1 small handful **Thai basil** and 1 tablespoon each **fish sauce** and **lime juice**.

green lentils

slow-cooked lamb shanks with lentils

Have your oven hot and ready at 160°C (315°F/Gas 2–3). Put 4 lamb shanks, 40 g (1 1/2 oz) chopped pancetta, 400 g (14 oz) tinned chopped tomatoes, 500 ml (17 fl oz/2 cups) beef or chicken stock, 250 ml (9 fl oz/1 cup) red wine, 100 g (3 1/2 oz/1/2 cup) green (puy) lentils and 2 bay leaves in a casserole dish, season well and cover with a tight-fitting lid. Cook in the oven for 2 1/2 hours, turning the shanks after 1 1/2 hours.

roasted lamb rack with marinated feta and lentils

Have your oven hot and ready at 180°C (350°F/Gas 4). Combine 100 g (3 1/4 oz/1/2 cup) green (puy) lentils in the bottom of a roasting pan with 1 chopped carrot, 1 chopped onion, 1 sliced celery stalk, 2 chopped garlic cloves and 500 ml (17 fl oz/2 cups) beef stock. Cook for 30 minutes then remove from the oven. Rub 75 g (2 1/2 oz/1/2 cup) marinated feta over 2 racks of lamb (6-cutlet). Sit the lamb on the lentils, grind over some black pepper and drizzle with 1 tablespoon of the tasty oil from the feta and cook in the oven for a further 20 minutes, until the cheese crust on the lamb is cooked golden. Allow the lamb to rest for 5 minutes before cutting and serving with the lentils.

lentil, chorizo and goat's cheese salad

Cook 200 g (7 oz/1 cup) green (puy) lentils in boiling water for 30 minutes. Meanwhile, cook 2 thinly sliced chorizos with a splash of olive oil in a hot pan for 4–5 minutes, stirring so the pieces cook to an even golden. Put the pieces and any of the tasty oil from the pan in a large bowl with 3 handfuls mixed salad leaf, 120 g (4 1/4 oz/1 cup) crumbled soft goat's cheese and the lentils. Mix up 2 tablespoons good olive oil, 2 tablespoons red wine vinegar and 1 teaspoon dijon mustard in a bowl and pour over the salad. Toss around to evenly combine the ingredients.

hoisin sauce is also used in a recipe on page... 169.

hoisin sauce

chinese barbecued pork

Toss 2 **pork loin fillets** in a bowl with 3 tablespoons **hoisin sauce**, 1 teaspoon **sesame oil**, 1 tablespoon **light soy sauce** and 1 tablespoon **soft brown sugar**, making sure the marinade is all over the meat. Leave for 30 minutes (or overnight in the refrigerator if you have the time). Have your oven hot and ready at 180°C (350°F/Gas 4). Place the pork on a rack over a baking tray. Pour 250 ml (9 fl oz/1 cup) water into the bottom of the tray and cook in the oven for 40 minutes, turning after 20 minutes. Allow to rest before serving warm with **steamed Chinese greens** or allow to cool and serve wrapped in little **Peking-duck-style pancakes** with sliced **cucumber** and **spring onion (scallion)**.

mongolian lamb cutlets

Put 12 **lamb cutlets** in a bowl with 125 ml (4 fl oz/^{1}/$_2$ cup) **hoisin sauce**, tossing them around to coat in the sauce. Heat a good few splashes of **vegetable oil** and ^{1}/$_2$ teaspoon **sesame oil** in a hot frying pan and cook the cutlets in batches for 1 minute each side. Remove the cutlets and cook 2 sliced **onions** for 6–8 minutes on a gentle heat, until really soft and well browned. Add 1 chopped **garlic clove** and 1 teaspoon grated **ginger** and cook for a minute to flavour the onions. Return the cutlets to the pan with 125 ml (4 fl oz/^{1}/$_2$ cup) **chicken stock** and 1 tablespoon **light soy sauce**. Let the liquid boil for 2–3 minutes, turning the cutlets in the boiling sauce, so they are glazed and coated in the sauce. Serve with **green beans** or **pumpkin (winter squash) mash**.

eggplant in chilli hoisin

Cut 1 **large eggplant (aubergine)** into 3 cm (1^1/$_4$ inch) pieces. Heat 3 tablespoons **vegetable oil** in a wok or frying pan. When the surface is shimmering, add the eggplant pieces and fry for 3–4 minutes, until golden. Remove and place on paper towel. Drain all but 1 teaspoon of oil from the pan and stir-fry 2 seeded and chopped **small red chillies**, 1 chopped **garlic clove**, 2 finely chopped **spring onions (scallions)** and 2 teaspoons grated **ginger** for a few seconds. Add 2 tablespoons **hoisin sauce**, 3 tablespoons **chicken stock** and a good pinch of **sugar** to the pan and boil for 2–3 minutes, until thickened slightly. Return the eggplant to the pan, gently toss through the sauce and serve with **rice** and **steamed Chinese greens**.

honey is also used in recipes on pages...
117, 123, 163 and 213.

honey

tofu with honey and black pepper

Heat 1 tablespoon **vegetable oil** in a saucepan on a high heat and cook 1 chopped **garlic clove** and 1 teaspoon grated **ginger** for a few seconds. Add 125 ml (4 fl oz/$^1/_2$ cup) **chicken stock**, 3 tablespoons **honey** and 1 teaspoon **black pepper** to the pan and boil for 4–5 minutes, until the mixture is syrupy. Cut a 600 g (1 lb 5 oz) block of **soft (silken) tofu** into 2–3 cm ($^3/_4$–1$^1/_4$ inch) cubes. Put the pieces on some paper towel to drain while you heat the oil to fry in. Heat 250 ml (9 fl oz/1 cup) **vegetable oil** in a wok. When the surface of the oil shimmers, dip half of the tofu in some **cornflour (cornstarch)**, shake off the excess and fry for 1–2 minutes, until nicely golden. Reheat to cook the remaining tofu. Put the cooked tofu on a plate, warm the honey sauce and pour over.

honey-and-spice lamb cutlets

Have your oven hot and ready at 220°C (425°F/Gas 7). Mix 3 tablespoons **honey**, 1 tablespoon **light soy sauce**, 1 tablespoon **lemon juice** and $^1/_2$ teaspoon **five-spice** in a bowl. Add 12 **lamb cutlets** and toss to coat evenly in the honey mixture. Heat a splash of **vegetable oil** in a non-stick frying pan over a medium–high heat. Cook the cutlets in batches for 1 minute each side (you may need to wipe the pan clean between batches), transfer to a baking tray and cook in the oven for 5 minutes (for medium–rare). Serve with **pumpkin (winter squash) mash** or **steamed greens**.

honey prawns

Heat 175 g (6 oz/$^1/_2$ cup) **honey** in a saucepan over a gentle heat until runny, and set aside. Heat 250 ml (9 fl oz/1 cup) **vegetable oil** in a wok. Combine 125 g (4$^1/_2$ oz/ 1 cup) **tempura flour** (available in the Asian section at supermarkets) with 250 ml (9 fl oz/1 cup) ice cold water until just combined but still a little lumpy. Dip 12 **raw large prawns (shrimp)**, 2 at a time, in the batter. Shake off excess batter and cook in the hot oil for 2–3 minutes and remove to a plate. Repeat with the remaining prawns. Quickly reheat the honey, pour over the prawns and sprinkle over 1 tablespoon lightly toasted **sesame seeds**.

hot pepper sauce is also used in recipes on pages...
63 and 103.

hot pepper sauce

spicy tomato rice

Blend 400 g (14 oz) tinned tomatoes, 1 chopped onion, 2 chopped garlic cloves and 1–2 teaspoons Tabasco (or another hot pepper sauce) in a food processor until smooth. Heat 2 tablespoons light olive oil in a saucepan and stir-fry 400 g (14 oz/2 cups) long-grain rice in the oil for 3–4 minutes. Add the tomato mixture and 750 ml (26 fl oz/3 cups) chicken stock and bring to the boil. Cover with a lid and reduce the heat to really low for 25 minutes. Remove from the heat and stir through 155 g (5 1/2 oz/1 cup) peas (defrosted if using frozen). Place the lid on for a further 5 minutes. Fluff the rice with a fork and stir through 1 large handful coriander (cilantro) leaves, roughly chopped. Season with salt and black pepper and serve.

tabasco mayonnaise

Put 3 egg yolks in a food processor with 2 teaspoons Tabasco (or another hot pepper sauce) and 1 teaspoon sea salt, and blend for a few seconds. With the motor running very slowly, add 250 ml (9 fl oz/1 cup) light olive oil, starting with a few drops at a time then gradually in a steady stream, until all the oil is incorporated and the mayonnaise is thick and creamy. You may add a squeeze of lime juice and a handful of coriander (cilantro) leaves, finely chopped. Enjoy as a dip for wedges, chargrilled chicken or a spicy addition to potato salad.

mexican baked beans

Cook 1 chopped onion, 2 chopped bacon slices and 1 sliced small red capsicum (pepper) in a splash of hot vegetable oil for 3–4 minutes, to soften the vegetables and crisp the bacon. Add 800 g (1 lb 12 oz) tinned baked beans and 1–2 teaspoons Tabasco (or another hot pepper sauce). Bring to the boil and simmer for 10 minutes, until the sauce has thickened. Serve at a picnic or with barbecued sausages.

indian curry paste is also used in recipes on pages...
81, 115, 147, 205 and 215.

indian curry paste

spinach and cheese curry

Cook 280 g (10 oz/2 cups) cubed **paneer** in a splash of sizzling **vegetable oil** in a non-stick frying pan for 2–3 minutes, until light golden. Remove to a plate and pour off any excess oil from the pan. Heat 40 g (1¹/₂ oz) **butter** in the pan and, when it is sizzles, add 2 tablespoons **mild Indian curry paste** (try madras or balti) and stir-fry for 2 minutes, to bring out all the hidden spices. Add 1 kg (2 lb 4 oz/2 bunches) roughly chopped **English spinach** to the pan and stir-fry for 3–4 minutes, until the spinach has totally wilted. Add 250 ml (9 fl oz/1 cup) **pouring (whipping) cream** to the pan, stirring to combine. Put the mixture in food processor and blend to a smooth paste. Return the sauce to the pan, add the cheese and heat gently for 2 minutes. Serve with **basmati rice**.

curry roast chicken

Have your oven hot and ready at 180°C (350°F/Gas 4) and put a baking tray to heat in the oven. Combine 60 g (2¹/₄ oz) softened **butter** with 2–3 tablespoons **mild Indian curry paste** (try madras). Wash and pat dry a **chicken**. Squeeze a **lemon** over the chicken and rub the juice into the skin. Rub half of the curry butter under the skin, between the skin and the breast meat, and smear the remaining butter all over the chicken. Place on the hot tray and roast for 1 hour and 10 minutes. Serve with **couscous, tomato and onion raita, mango chutney** and **minted yoghurt**.

madras rack of lamb

Have your oven hot and ready at 220°C (425°F/Gas 7) and put a baking tray to heat in the oven. Blend 3 tablespoons **madras curry paste** (or another mild Indian curry paste), 125 g (4¹/₂ oz/¹/₂ cup) **plain yoghurt** and 1 large handful **coriander (cilantro) leaves** in a food processor to make a smooth, spiced and tangy paste. Rub the paste over 2 **racks of lamb (6-cutlet)** and spinkle over 1 teaspoon **sea salt** and lots of **black pepper**. Place the racks on the hot tray and into the oven for 20 minutes for pink lamb, 5 minutes more for medium. Remove from the oven and wrap in foil for 5 minutes before cutting into individual cutlets. Squeeze over some **lemon juice** and serve as individual pieces or 3–4 cutlets each as a meal.

jam is also used in recipes on pages...
227 and 209.

jam

jam cake

Have your oven hot and ready at 180°C (350°F/Gas 4). Grease a 25 cm (10 inch) bundt cake tin. Put 185 g (6½ oz) softened **butter** and 185 g (6½ oz/1 cup) **soft brown sugar** in a food processor and blend until smooth. Add 3 **eggs**, one at a time, and blend for a few seconds between each addition. Add 250 g (9 oz/1 cup) **sour cream** or **crème fraîche** and 250 g (9 oz/2 cups) **self-raising flour** to the food processor and blend until you have a thick batter. Stir through 315 g (11 oz/1 cup) **jam**, spoon into the tin and bake for 45 minutes. Serve warm with **ice cream** or **custard**.

raspberry and croissant puddings

Have your oven hot and ready at 220°C (425°F/Gas 7). Grease 4 250 ml (9 fl oz/1 cup) ovenproof dishes. Cut 2 small **croissants** crossways into thin slices and spread a little **raspberry jam** on one side of each slice. Divide the slices between the dishes, placing in layers. Put 300 ml (10½ fl oz) **pouring (whipping) cream**, 100 ml (3½ fl oz) **milk** and 2 tablespoons **custard powder** in a small saucepan and whisk over a gentle heat for a few minutes, until slightly thickened. Pour the custard mix over the croissant slices and bake for 15 minutes, until the edges are golden and look set. The custard may still be deliciously soft underneath. Allow to cool a little before serving.

hot jam and coconut tarts

Have your oven hot and ready at 220°C (425°F/Gas 7) and place a baking tray in the oven. Place 4 **mini sweet tart cases** (try Pampas, leaving the pastry in the foil case) on the hot tray and bake for 8–10 minutes, until the crimped edges of the tart shell turn golden. Remove and put 1 tablespoon **jam** (any berry flavour works best) and a sprinkling of **desiccated coconut** on top and return to the oven for 4–5 minutes, until the coconut turns golden. Allow to cool a little then serve with some **whipped cream** or **vanilla ice cream**.

kidney beans are also used in a recipe on page...
99.

kidney beans

spiced potato and bean salad

Cook 2 peeled and cubed **potatoes** in boiling water for 10 minutes. Drain well. Heat 2 tablespoons **vegetable oil** in a frying pan and cook 2 finely sliced **red onions** and 1 chopped **large green chilli** for 3–4 minutes, to soften the onions. Add the potatoes to the pan with 1 teaspoon **sea salt** and 1 teaspoon **ground cumin**. Stir-fry for 4–5 minutes. Put the spiced potatoes in a bowl with 400 g (14 oz) tinned **kidney beans**, rinsed and drained, 1 tablespoon **lemon juice**, a good grinding of **black pepper** and a large handful of **coriander (cilantro) leaves**. Toss to combine and serve.

indian kidney bean curry

Cook 1 chopped **onion** and 1 chopped **garlic clove** in a splash of **vegetable oil** for 2–3 minutes, so the onion softens. Add 1/2 teaspoon each **ground cumin** and **chilli powder** and stir-fry for a minute. Add 400 g (14 oz) tinned **tomatoes** and 500 ml (17 fl oz/ 2 cups) water and boil for 10 minutes. Add 400 g (14 oz) tinned **kidney beans**, rinsed and drained, and a handful of **coriander (cilantro) leaves** and simmer for 5 minutes. Serve with **basmati rice, poppadoms** and **cucumber** slices.

smoky bean nachos

Cook 300 g (10 1/2 oz) finely chopped **smoked pork sausage** and 1 chopped **onion** in a splash of sizzling **olive oil** for 4–5 minutes, so the sausage starts to turn golden. Add 1 teaspoon **dried thyme**, 400 g (14 oz) tinned **kidney beans**, rinsed and drained, 400 g (14 oz) tinned **chopped tomatoes**, 125 ml (4 fl oz/ 1/2 cup) water and boil for 5 minutes, until thickened. Season well with **salt** and **black pepper**. Serve over warmed **corn chips** or wrapped in **tortilla** with grated **cheddar** and **guacamole** or **sour cream** on the side.

lime pickle

lime pickle, coriander and soy swordfish

Put 4 tablespoons lime pickle in a food processor with 1 tablespoon light olive oil, 1 large handful coriander (cilantro) leaves, 2 tablespoons lemon juice and 2 tablespoons soy sauce and blend to a smooth paste. Place in a shallow dish with 4 swordfish steaks, rubbing the paste evenly all over the fish. Cover and set aside for 10 minutes, or refrigerate for a few hours. Heat a grill plate or barbecue to very hot and cook for 2–3 minutes each side. Serve with a simple green salad, pilaff, couscous or vegetable curry.

zesty lime pickle rice

Heat a splash of vegetable oil in a saucepan and stir-fry 1 chopped onion for 2–3 minutes, until softened. Add 3 tablespoons finely chopped lime pickle and a good grinding of black pepper to the pan and cook for a couple of minutes to bring out the hidden aromatics in the pickle. Add 200 g (7 oz/1 cup) long-grain rice (try basmati or jasmine) and stir around for 2 minutes to coat all the grains in the seasonings. Pour in 500 ml (17 fl oz/2 cups) water or chicken stock (for more flavour), stir once and bring to the boil. Reduce the heat to low and cover the pan with a tight-fitting lid. Cook for 20 minutes then remove the pan from the heat and leave the lid on for a further 5 minutes. Stir through 2 tablespoons lime juice and a handful of chopped coriander (cilantro) leaves, fluffing up with a fork.

pumpkin with lime pickle dressing

Combine 2 tablespoons finely chopped lime pickle, 1 tablespoon tamari or light soy sauce, a pinch of sugar and 1 tablespoon water until smooth. Cook 450 g (1 lb/ 3 cups) peeled and cubed pumpkin (winter squash) in boiling water for 10 minutes, until cooked through but still firm. Drain well and toss the warm pumpkin in a bowl with the lime pickle sauce, 1 large handful coriander (cilantro) leaves, chopped, and some black pepper.

long-grain rice is also used in recipes on pages...
121, 137, 145 and 203.

long-grain rice

prawn, leek and pine nut fried rice

Beat 2 **eggs** in a large bowl and add 555–740 g (1 lb 4 oz–1 lb 10 oz/ 3–4 cups) **cooked long-grain white rice**, stirring around to evenly combine the rice with the egg. Heat 3 tablespoons **vegetable oil** in a hot wok and stir-fry 2 sliced **leeks**, 80 g (2³/4 oz/¹/2 cup) **pine nuts** and 2 crushed **garlic cloves** for a few seconds, so the nuts start to turn golden and the leeks soften. Add 24 peeled and deveined **raw small prawns (shrimp)** and stir-fry for 2 minutes, so the prawns turn pink and curly. Add the rice mixture with 1 teaspoon **sea salt** and stir-fry for 4–5 minutes, constantly tossing the rice to evenly combine the flavours.

ham and egg fried rice

Beat 4 **eggs** in a large bowl and add 555–740 g (1 lb 4 oz–1 lb 10 oz/ 3–4 cups) **cooked long-grain white rice**, stirring around to evenly combine the rice with the egg. Heat 3 tablespoons **light cooking oil** and 1 teaspoon **sesame oil** in a wok or large frying pan and stir-fry 310 g (11 oz/ 2 cups) **sliced ham** for 2–3 minutes, so the ham crisps and flavours the oil nicely. Add 4 finely sliced **spring onions (scallions)** and stir-fry for a few seconds. Add the rice to the wok and stir-fry for 5–6 minutes, so the egg cooks and starts to brown. Stir through 1 tablespoon **light soy sauce** and 155 g (5¹/2 oz/1 cup) **peas** (defrosted if using frozen), cook for 1–2 minutes and serve.

chicken biryani

Have your oven hot and ready at 180°C (350°F/Gas 4). Cook 400 g (14 oz/2 cups) **basmati rice** and 2 teaspoons **turmeric** in boiling water for 5 minutes and drain well. Heat a splash of **olive oil** and 20 g (³/4 oz) **butter** in a casserole dish. When the butter sizzles, add 1 sliced **red onion** and stir-fry for 5 minutes, so the onion starts to darken. Add 2 tablespoons **mild Indian curry paste** and stir-fry for a minute, to bring out the spices in the paste. Add 2 **skinless, boneless chicken breasts**, cut into bite-sized pieces, and stir-fry for 2 minutes. Add the rice to the dish and stir around well to coat the rice in the spicy oil. Add 500 ml (17 fl oz/2 cups) **chicken stock**, bring the mixture to the boil and cover with a tight-fitting lid. Cook in the oven for 40 minutes and serve with **yoghurt** and **lemon wedges**.

long pasta is also used in recipes on pages...
19, 27, 41, 47, 75, 93, 105 and 197.

long pasta

the easiest spaghetti sauce

Cook 400 g (14 oz) **spaghetti** in boiling water for 8–10 minutes. Drain and return to the warm pan. Meanwhile, put 3 tablespoons good **olive oil**, 4 chopped ripe and tasty **tomatoes**, 2 teaspoons rinsed **small capers**, 2 **anchovy fillets** and 1 chopped **garlic clove** in a saucepan and cook over a gentle heat for 3–4 minutes, just to soften everything. Toss the sauce and the spaghetti together and season well. Serve with grated **parmesan**.

smoked chicken linguine

Cook 400 g (14 oz) **linguine** in boiling water for 8–10 minutes. Drain well and return to the warm pan. Meanwhile, stir-fry 1 sliced **red capsicum (pepper)** in a frying pan with a splash of **olive oil** for 2–3 minutes, so the capsicum gently softens but doesn't brown in the oil. Add 250 ml (9 fl oz/ 1 cup) **pouring (whipping) cream** and boil for 5 minutes, so the cream thickens slightly. Add 350 g (12 oz/2 cups) shredded **smoked chicken** (or leftover turkey), 1 tablespoon rinsed **capers** and a handful of roughly chopped **flat-leaf (Italian) parsley**. Add to the pasta with 50 g (1³/4 oz/ ¹/2 cup) grated **parmesan** and a good grinding of **black pepper** and stir to evenly coat the pasta in the sauce.

spaghetti with fried sardines, parsley and lemon

Cook 400 g (14 oz) **spaghetti** in boiling water for 8–10 minutes. Drain well and return to the pot. Meanwhile, heat 3 tablespoons good **olive oil** in a frying pan and add 105 g (3³/4 oz) tinned **sardines**, drained of oil, and cook for a few minutes over a high heat so the sardines start to brown and crisp. Add 3 chopped **garlic cloves** and 1 chopped **small red chilli** (optional) and cook for a few more minutes so the garlic browns nicely, but doesn't burn. Add a handful of chopped **flat-leaf (Italian) parsley** and 2 tablespoons **lemon juice**. Add the sauce to the pasta, toss and season well. Serve with some grated **parmesan** on the side.

madeira cake

sicilian grape and mascarpone cake

Cut a **madeira (pound) cake** in half through the middle. Whip together 3 tablespoons **mascarpone**, 125 ml (4 fl oz/1/2 cup) **pouring (whipping) cream** and 3 tablespoons **icing (confectioners') sugar** in a bowl until smooth. Spread over the cake, top with 180 g (6^{1}/2 oz/1 cup) **red grapes** and sift over some extra **icing sugar**. Double the mixture to make 2 cakes or save the other half of the cake for a trifle or tiramisu.

tiramisu

Roughly break up a **madeira (pound) cake** to give 3 cups of large chunks and place the pieces in a small ceramic dish. Combine 3 tablespoons **espresso coffee** with 3 tablespoons **Marsala** or **dark rum** and pour over the sponge. Beat 3 **egg yolks** with 110 g (3^{3}/4 oz/1/2 cup) **mascarpone**, 250 ml (9 fl oz/1 cup) **pouring (whipping) cream** and 3 tablespoons **sugar** until smooth and thick. Beat 3 **egg whites** until you have firm peaks and fold into the cream mixture. Spoon over the cake and sprinkle with 1 tablespoon **unsweetened cocoa powder**. Enjoy straight away or refrigerate until needed.

strawberry and passionfruit trifle

Cover the bottom of a small ceramic dish with 1 cm (3/4 inch) thick slices of **madeira (pound) cake**. Pour over 3 tablespoons **sweet sherry** then pour over 250 ml (9 fl oz/1 cup) **ready-made custard**. Toss 250 g (9 oz) halved **strawberries** and 3 tablespoons **passionfruit pulp** in a bowl and spoon evenly over the custard. Beat 250 ml (9 fl oz/1 cup) **pouring (whipping) cream** with 2 tablespoons **icing (confectioners') sugar** to form soft peaks and spoon over the fruit. Top with a sprinkling of lightly toasted **flaked almonds**.

maple syrup is also used in recipes on pages...
41, 61 and 163.

maple syrup

five-spice maple glazed pork

Combine 3 tablespoons **maple syrup**, 1 tablespoon **dark soy sauce** and 1 teaspoon **five-spice** in a dish and add 8 **pork spare ribs**. (about 12 cm/4½ inches long). Toss the pork around to coat in the syrupy mix. Have a grill plate or frying pan hot and ready to go. Add a splash of **light cooking oil** and cook the pork for 4 minutes each side (reduce the heat if the pork begins to burn). Remove from the heat and allow to rest on a plate for a few minutes. Serve on a bed of some blanched **broccolini** (or your favourite greens) and **rice**.

maple custard

Whisk together 125 ml (4 fl oz/ ½ cup) **maple syrup**, 250 ml (9 fl oz/1 cup) **pouring (whipping) cream** and 3 **egg yolks** in a heatproof bowl. Bring a small saucepan of water to a rapid simmer and place the bowl on top. Cook over the simmering water for 8–10 minutes, stirring pretty much all the time, until the custard is silky smooth and thickened. Take the bowl off the water and set aside. If you cover the top of the custard with some plastic wrap at this point, it will prevent a skin forming on top. Enjoy spooned over **grilled peaches** or a **berry fruit salad**.

maple pears

Put 250 ml (9 fl oz/1 cup) **maple syrup**, 250 ml (9 fl oz/1 cup) water, 1 **cinnamon stick** and 2 **cloves** in a saucepan and bring to the boil. Add 4 peeled, cored and quartered **pears** and simmer for 20 minutes. Allow the pears to cool in the mixture and serve with **ice cream** or **mascarpone**, or thinly slice and serve with a cheese platter.

marmalade

three ways with

orange and chilli ribs

Bring a large pot of water to boil. Add 16 **American-style pork ribs** and cook for 10 minutes. Drain and place in a bowl. Combine 250 ml (9 fl oz/1 cup) **chicken stock**, 3 tablespoons **orange marmalade**, 1 tablespoon **fish sauce** and 1 tablespoon **dark soy sauce** in a bowl. Heat a splash of **light cooking oil** in a really hot wok and stir-fry the pork ribs for 3–4 minutes. Add 1^1/$_2$ teaspoons **chilli flakes** and 1 teaspoon **ground coriander** and stir-fry for a minute. Pour the sauce mixture in and boil for 10–15 minutes, until syrupy and thickly coating the ribs. Serve as a finger-food starter.

star anise and orange duck

Chop a **Chinese barbecued duck** into 10–12 pieces. Boil 250 ml (9 fl oz/1 cup) **rice wine**, 250 ml (9 fl oz/1 cup) **chicken stock**, 160 g (5^3/4 oz/^{1}/$_2$ cup) **marmalade**, 2 tablespoons **fish sauce**, 2 **star anise** and 1 **cinnamon stick** in a saucepan for 10 minutes. Add the duck and cook on a rapid simmer for 15 minutes so the sauce really thickens and coats the duck pieces. Serve with **rice** and **steamed Chinese greens**.

ginger and marmalade bread puddings

Have your oven hot and ready at 180°C (350°F/Gas 4). **Butter** 4 slices of **white bread** (crusts removed) then generously spread each slice with **marmalade**. Place the bread to fit snugly in a well-buttered 1 litre (35 fl oz/4 cup) baking dish. Combine 500 ml (17 fl oz/2 cups) **pouring (whipping) cream**, 3 **eggs**, 2 tablespoons **sugar** and 1 teaspoon **ground ginger**, and pour over the bread. Sprinkle **sugar** over the top and bake for 40–45 minutes until puffed and golden. Serve with **custard** or **ice cream**.

meringues are also used in recipes on pages...
61 and 69.

meringues

banoffee meringue pie

Break 8 small meringues (about
8 cm/3 1/4 inches across) into
bite-sized pieces and place in
a ceramic pie dish. Heat 60 g
(2 1/4 oz) butter, 140 g (5 oz/3/4 cup)
soft brown sugar and 250 ml
(9 fl oz/1 cup) thick (double/
heavy) cream in a saucepan and
stir over a gentle heat until it
is totally smooth and looks like
caramel velvet. Remove from the
heat and allow to cool to room
temperature, when it will thicken
a little. Thinly slice 4 bananas over
the meringues and spoon the
caramel over the top. Beat 300 ml
(10 1/2 fl oz) pouring (whipping)
cream with 2 tablespoons icing
(confectioners') sugar until the
mixture has thickened to firm
peaks. Spoon over the bananas
and sprinkle 40 g (1 1/2 oz/1/4 cup)
chopped peanuts on top.

tropical pav

Break 6–8 small meringues (about
8 cm/3 1/4 inches across) into large
pieces and place them in a serving
dish. Lightly beat 125 ml (4 fl oz/
1/2 cup) pouring (whipping)
cream with 2 tablespoons icing
(confectioners') sugar to form soft
peaks. Spoon the cream over the
meringues. Top with 2 thinly sliced
bananas, a cubed mango and
cover the fruit with 3 tablespoons
passionfruit pulp.

drunken chocolate
ice cream meringues

Break a 200 g (7 oz) block of dark
chocolate into small pieces. Pour
3 tablespoons thick (double/
heavy) cream in a saucepan and
stir over a gentle heat until it is
almost about to boil. Add the
chocolate, piece by piece, to
the hot cream, stirring until all
the chocolate is incorporated
and the sauce is silky smooth.
Remove from the heat and stir
in 3 tablespoons Grand Marnier
or Frangelico. Cut the tops off
4 individual meringues, spoon a
big scoop of vanilla ice cream
onto each one and generously
pour the indulgent sauce over.

miso

three ways with

slow-cooked miso and ginger pork belly

Have your oven hot and ready at 160°C (315°F/Gas 2–3). Heat 1 tablespoon **vegetable oil** in a heavy-based frying pan. Cook a 500–600 g (1 lb 2 oz–1 lb 5 oz) piece of **pork belly**, skin side down, in the smoking hot oil for 2–3 minutes, so the skin is golden. Cook for a minute each on the other sides. Place the pork, skin side down, and 6 slices of **ginger** in a casserole dish. Combine 500 ml (17 fl oz/2 cups) hot water with 4 tablespoons **miso paste** and 2 tablespoons **soft brown sugar**. Stir to dissolve the miso and pour over the pork. Cover with a tight-fitting lid and cook in the oven for 2½ hours, turning after 1 hour. Remove the pork from the hot liquid and allow to cool for 10 minutes. Boil 250 ml (9 fl oz/ 1 cup) of the sauce for 5 minutes, to thicken a little. Slice the pork and serve with **rice** and some of the sauce poured over.

silky leek and miso risotto

Boil 1 litre (35 fl oz/4 cups) water and add 1 teaspoon **dashi granules** and 1 tablespoon **miso paste**. Reduce the heat to a low simmer. Cook 2 finely sliced **leeks** and 1 chopped **garlic clove** in 40 g (1½ oz) of gently sizzling **butter** for 5 minutes, stirring often, so the leeks are silky soft. Add 220 g (7¾ oz/1 cup) **short-grain** or **arborio rice**, stir for a minute then add 125 ml (4 fl oz/½ cup) of the hot stock. Stir until almost all the liquid has been absorbed and repeat the process until all the stock has been used. This may take about 25 minutes. Stir through 50 g (1¾ oz/½ cup) grated **parmesan**, a handful of finely chopped **flat-leaf (Italian) parsley** and an extra 20 g (¾ oz) **butter**. Serve with a little extra **parmesan** on top.

miso and lemon thyme crumbed lamb fillets

Rub 2 tablepoons **miso paste** evenly over 2 **large lamb backstrap** or **loin fillets**. Combine 100 g (3½ oz/1 cup) **breadcrumbs** (if you can get your hands on them, try using the excellent Japanese breadcrumbs, panko) with 1 teaspoon finely chopped **lemon thyme** and a small handful of **flat-leaf (Italian) parsley**, finely chopped. Roll the lamb in the crumb mix, pressing down firmly to evenly coat the lamb. Heat a couple of splashes of **light olive oil** in a frying pan and cook the fillets in the sizzling hot oil for 3–4 minutes each side (or 1 minute each side if using loin fillets). Remove and allow to rest for a couple of minutes before slicing on an angle and serving with **pumpkin (winter squash) mash** or a **baby English spinach leaf salad**.

mustard is also used in recipes on pages...
13, 21, 23, 37, 43, 103, 105, 131 and 183.

mustard

mustard and herb crumbed veal cutlets

Smear 2 tablepoons of your favourite **mustard** over 4 **veal cutlets**. Combine 80 g (2 3/4 oz/ 1 cup) **breadcrumbs**, 1 teaspoon each **dried oregano** and **dried basil** in a bowl with a good pinch of **salt** and **black pepper**. Press the crumb mixture firmly into each veal cutlet, to cover all over. Heat some **light olive oil** and 40 g (1 1/2 oz) **butter** over a gentle heat, so the butter bubbles. Add the cutlets and cook for 6 minutes each side, until a golden crust is formed. Serve with **pumpkin (winter squash)** mash, coleslaw or **green salad**.

tomato, basil and mustard tart

Have your oven hot and ready at 220°C (425°F/Gas 7). Fold over the edges of a sheet of frozen **puff pastry** to make a 1 cm (1/2 inch) border and press down with the back of a fork. Place on a baking tray lined with baking paper and bake for 10 minutes. Remove and spread 1 tablespoon **mild mustard** over the hot tart and lay 2 finely sliced ripe and tasty **tomatoes** on the tart. Season well, drizzle with good **olive oil** and return to the oven for 8–10 minutes, so the tart is really golden and the tomatoes warm and soft. Sprinkle a handful of chopped **kalamata olives** and a handful of torn **basil** over the tart, cut into quarters and enjoy as a starter.

potato salad with mustard basil dressing

Put 125 g (4 1/2 oz/1/2 cup) good **mayonnaise** in a food processor with 2 tablespoons **mild mustard**, 2 chopped **garlic cloves** and 1 handful **basil** and process until the basil is chopped finely in the mixture. Put 12 **baby potatoes** (try nicola) in a saucepan and cover with cold water. Place on a high heat. As soon as the water boils, remove from the heat and place on a tight-fitting lid for 20 minutes. Drain and toss the warm potatoes in the dressing. Season well and serve at a barbecue.

oats

three ways with

creamy oat and raspberry pudding

Place 100 g (3^1/$_2$ oz/1 cup) **rolled (porridge) oats** in a frying pan and cook over a gentle heat, shaking the pan constantly for a few minutes so they warm through evenly. Put in a bowl and allow to cool. Add 125 ml (4 fl oz/^{1}/$_2$ cup) **thickened (whipping) cream**, 1 tablespoon **honey** and 2 tablespoons **icing (confectioners') sugar** to the oats and stir to evenly combine. Fold through 150 g (5^1/$_2$ oz/1 cup) defrosted frozen **raspberries**. Serve with some extra **honey** drizzled over.

coconut, maple and pecan granola

Place 200 g (7 oz/2 cups) **rolled (porridge) oats**, 45 g (1^1/$_2$ oz/^{1}/$_2$ cup) **desiccated coconut** and 125 g (4^1/$_2$ oz/1 cup) chopped **pecans** in a baking tray and cook in a hot oven for 10 minutes, occasionally stirring the oats from the edge into the centre so they cook and golden evenly. Stir 3 tablespoons **maple syrup** through the hot mixture and return to the oven for just a few minutes. Stir well so the sweet maple syrup coats the ingredients. Store in a container and enjoy with **yoghurt** or **milk**, or stir through **dried blueberries**.

apple crumble

Have your oven hot and ready at 220°C (425°F/Gas 7). Peel and slice 3 **apples** directly into a saucepan with 20 g (^{3}/$_4$ oz) **butter**, 1 tablespoon **sugar** and 1 teaspoon **natural vanilla extract** and cook for 5–6 minutes, to soften the apples. Place the apples in an ovenproof dish. Put 50 g (1^3/$_4$ oz/^{1}/$_2$ cup) **rolled (porridge) oats**, 60 g (2^1/$_4$ oz/^{1}/$_2$ cup) **plain (all-purpose) flour**, 3 tablespoons **soft brown sugar** and 40 g (1^1/$_2$ oz) cold **butter** in a food processor and blend until the mixture looks like coarse breadcrumbs. Sprinkle over the fruit and bake for 10 minutes, just until the top goes golden. Enjoy with **vanilla ice cream** or **custard**.

oyster sauce is also used in recipes on pages...
29, 33, 51, 125, 173 and 185.

oyster sauce

stir-fried beef with broccolini and oyster sauce

Finely slice 500 g (1 lb 2 oz) **rump steak** or **beef fillet** across the grain and toss around in a bowl with 1 tablespoon **rice wine** (or white wine) and 1 tablespoon **light soy sauce**. Set aside for 10 minutes. Heat 3 tablespoons **vegetable oil** in a wok until smoking hot and stir-fry half of the beef for 1 minute. Remove the beef to a plate, reheat the oil and repeat with the remaining beef. Drain all but 1 tablespoon of oil from the wok and stir-fry 4 sliced **spring onions (scallions)**, 2 chopped **garlic cloves** and 1 teaspoon grated **ginger** for a few seconds. Add 2 bunches roughly chopped **broccolini** and stir-fry for 2–3 minutes. Return the beef to the wok with 3 tablespoons each **oyster sauce** and water, a pinch of **sugar** and a small splash of **sesame oil**. Boil for 2 minutes and serve with **rice**.

san choy bau of pork, mushroom and water chestnut

Soak 4 **dried Chinese mushrooms** in boiling water for 20 minutes. Cut off the stems and slice the caps, and keep 3 tablespoons of the soaking liquid. Add 2 tablespoons **vegetable oil** to a really hot wok and stir-fry 2 **garlic cloves** and 2 teaspoons finely grated **ginger** for just a few seconds. Add 500 g (1 lb 2 oz) **minced (ground) pork** and stir-fry for 5 minutes, so it browns evenly. Add the mushroom liquid, 3 tablespoons water, 3 tablespoons **oyster sauce** and 90 g (3 1/4 oz/ 1/2 cup) chopped **water chestnuts** to the wok and bring to the boil for a few minutes, so the sauce thickens. Sprinkle over some sliced **spring onions (scallions)** and serve in fresh **butter lettuce leaves**.

slow braised gingered beef

Toss 600 g (1 lb 5 oz) **chuck** or **stewing steak**, chopped into 3 cm (1 1/4 inch) pieces, in a bowl with 125 ml (4 fl oz/ 1/2 cup) **oyster sauce** and 1/2 teaspoon **black pepper**. Heat 2 tablespoons **light cooking oil** in a casserole dish over a high heat and cook the beef in batches for 4–5 minutes, turning often so the meat is nicely browned, and set aside. Add 6–8 thick slices of **ginger** to the pan with 4–6 **garlic cloves** and 1 sliced **onion**. Cook for a few minutes to soften the onion then add 750 ml (26 fl oz/3 cups) **chicken stock** and bring to the boil. Return the meat to the pan, cover and simmer over a low heat for 1 hour. Remove the lid and bring to a rapid boil for 10 minutes, to thicken the sauce, and serve with **rice**.

panettone

three ways with

plum bruschetta

Halve 8 **plums** and remove the stones. Toss the plums in 2 tablespoons **soft brown sugar**. Cook the plums in 20 g ($^3/_4$ oz) of gently sizzling **butter** and add 2 tablespoons **orange juice** to the pan, shaking the pan so the plums soften. Remove from the heat. Toast 4 thick slices of **panettone** until lightly golden and spread each piece generously with **fresh ricotta**. Spoon the plums and any juices over the top and dust with **icing (confectioners')** sugar.

italian bread and butter pudding

Have your oven hot and ready at 180°C (350°F/Gas 4). Grease a 1–1.5 litre (35–52 fl oz/4–6 cup) baking dish. Cut 4–6 slices of **panettone**, then tear each slice into 2–3 smaller pieces. Spread **butter** on both sides of the bread and lay the pieces in the dish. Beat 4 **eggs**, 3 tablespoons **caster (superfine) sugar**, 500 ml (17 fl oz/2 cups) **milk** and 125 ml (4 fl oz/$^1/_2$ cup) **pouring (whipping) cream** in a bowl and pour over the bread. Allow to sit for 10 minutes then bake in the oven for 45–50 minutes, until puffed and golden. Serve warm with **ice cream**.

panettone french toast

Beat 4 **eggs**, 125 ml (4 fl oz/$^1/_2$ cup) **pouring (whipping) cream** and 125 ml (4 fl oz/$^1/_2$ cup) **milk** in a bowl. Cut 4 thick wedges from a **panettone** then cut each wedge in half. Heat 20 g ($^3/_4$ oz) **butter** in a non-stick frying pan so it gently sizzles, being careful not to burn the butter. Dip 2 slices of panettone in the egg mix, turning over several times so the slices become soggy. Cook for 2 minutes each side, so the egg sets around the edge and the toast is dark golden. Add more butter to the pan and repeat with the remaining bread. Serve with **fresh berries**.

peanuts are also used in recipes on pages...
115, 129 and 157.

peanuts

dry, spicy peanut chicken curry

Blend 80 g (2 3/4 oz/1/2 cup) peanuts in a food processor until finely chopped. Toss 6 quartered chicken thigh fillets, 1 teaspoon finely chopped bottled green peppercorns and 2 tablespoons plain (all-purpose) flour around in a bowl, to evenly coat the chicken. Heat 3 tablespoons peanut oil in a frying pan and stir-fry the chicken pieces for 3–4 minutes, to just brown. Remove the chicken, leaving a tablespoon of oil in the pan. Stir-fry 2 tablespoons red curry paste in the pan for 1 minute, to release all the hidden spices in the paste. Add 1 tablespoon soft brown sugar, 250 ml (9 fl oz/1 cup) coconut milk, 2 tablespoons fish sauce and the peanuts. Boil for 8–10 minutes, until really thick. Return the chicken to the pan with 1 small handful Thai basil and cook for 2–3 minutes on a gentle heat, stirring to coat the chicken in the thick spicy sauce.

gunpowder chicken

Heat 3 tablespoons vegetable oil in a hot wok. Add 4 quartered chicken thigh fillets and cook for 2–3 minutes each side, so the chicken is golden and crispy. Remove the chicken and drain all but 1 tablespoon of oil from the wok. Stir-fry 1 chopped garlic clove, 1 teaspoon chilli flakes, 4 spring onions (scallions), chopped into 3 cm (1 1/4 inch) lengths, and 2 teaspoons grated ginger and stir-fry for a few seconds. Add 1 sliced red capsicum (pepper) and 80 g (2 3/4 oz/1/2 cup) unsalted peanuts. Stir-fry for a minute and return the chicken to the wok with 3 tablespoons hoisin sauce, 125 ml (4 fl oz/1/2 cup) chicken stock and 1/2 teaspoon sugar. Bring to a rapid boil for a few minutes, until the sauce is thick and coats all the ingredients. Serve with rice.

thai peanut pesto

Blend 80 g (2 3/4 oz/1/2 cup) peanuts, 1 handful mint, 1 handful basil (preferably Thai basil), 1 handful coriander (cilantro) leaves, 1 seeded small red chilli, 2 tablespoons lime juice, 2 tablespoons fish sauce and 1 tablespoon shaved palm sugar or soft brown sugar in a food processor until smooth. Serve dolloped on sweet potato soup, with roasted pumpkin (winter squash) or tossed through Asian noodles and roast chicken.

peanut butter

three ways with

satay sauce

Combine 250 g (9 oz/1 cup) peanut butter, 1 tablespoon soft brown sugar, 250 ml (9 fl oz/ 1 cup) coconut milk, 1 chopped small red chilli (remove the seeds for a less spicy satay) and a good squeeze of lemon juice in a small saucepan. Bring the mixture to a gentle simmer for 5 minutes, stirring often so the sauce is smooth and thick. Serve over steamed green beans, bean sprouts and sliced hard-boiled eggs for a Javanese-style vegetable salad.

spicy peanut beef with fragrant thai basil

Boil half the coconut milk from a 400 ml (14 fl oz) tin in a frying pan for 5 minutes, stirring often. Add 2–3 tablespoons red curry paste and stir-fry for 2–3 minutes. Add 2 tablespoons peanut butter, 1 tablespoon fish sauce and 1 tablespoon soft brown sugar and cook for 2–3 minutes, stirring constantly to combine. Add the remaining tinned coconut milk. When the mixture boils, add 600 g (1 lb 5 oz) rump steak, sliced into thin strips, cover and cook over a gentle simmer for 5 minutes. Stir through 1 large handful Thai basil and serve with jasmine rice. Top with extra Thai basil and a finely sliced large red chilli.

stir-fried vegetables with peanut noodles

Cover 200 g (7 oz) rice stick noodles with boiling water for 8 minutes then drain well. Combine 3 tablespoons crunchy peanut butter, 2 tablespoons tamarind purée and 1 tablespoon soft brown sugar with 185 ml (6 fl oz/3/4 cup) hot water. Heat a generous splash of vegetable oil in a wok or frying pan and stir-fry 2 chopped garlic cloves and 2 teaspoons grated ginger for just a few seconds to flavour the oil. Add 120 g (4 1/4 oz/2 cups) broccoli florets and 1 sliced small red capsicum (pepper) and stir–fry for 2–3 minutes. Add 2 handfuls bean sprouts and stir-fry for 2 minutes, so the sprouts wilt. Add the noodles and sauce mixture to the pan and stir-fry for 4–5 minutes, so the noodles and vegetables are evenly coated in the sauce.

pine nuts are also used in recipes on pages...
39, 47, 91, 147 and 183.

pine nuts

shell pasta with chilli, pine nuts and broccolini

Cook 400 g (14 oz) **small shell pasta** in boiling water for 8–10 minutes. In the last 2 minutes of cooking add 1 bunch **broccolini**, cut into 3 cm (1¼ inch) lengths, to the water. Drain well and return to the saucepan. Meanwhile, heat a splash of **olive oil** and 60 g (2¼ oz) **butter** in a frying pan over a medium heat. When the butter sizzles, add 4 tablespoons **pine nuts** and 1 teaspoon **chilli flakes**, shaking the pan to evenly brown the pine nuts. Pour over the pasta, add 50 g (1¾ oz/½ cup) finely grated **parmesan** or **ricotta**, season well and toss to evenly combine. Serve with some extra **parmesan** on top, or toss through some **ricotta** to taste.

persian lamb pizza

Have your oven hot and ready at 220°C (425°F/Gas 7). Heat a splash of **olive oil** in a frying pan and cook 1 sliced **onion** and 2 chopped **garlic cloves** for 4–5 minutes in the sizzling oil, until golden. Add 1 teaspoon each **ground cumin**, **ground coriander** and **sea salt**, and cook for 1 minute. Add 300 g (10½ oz) **minced (ground) lamb** and stir-fry for 5 minutes, until evenly browned. Spread the lamb mixture over a round piece of **pitta bread**, top with 3 tablespoons **pine nuts** and cook in the oven for 5–8 minutes, so the bread crisps up and the nuts are golden. Enjoy with a **green salad** and some **hummus** on the side. Serves 2.

spicy chicken and pine nut san choy bau

Heat a splash of **vegetable oil** in a wok or frying pan and stir-fry 3 tablespoons **pine nuts**, 2 chopped **garlic cloves** and 1 seeded and chopped **small red chilli** for a few seconds until aromatic and the pine nuts start to turn golden. Add 500 g (1 lb 2 oz) **minced (ground) chicken** and stir-fry for 5 minutes, so the chicken browns evenly. Add 2 tablespoons **oyster sauce**, 1 tablespoon **light soy sauce** and a good pinch of **sugar** to the pan and stir-fry for a few more minutes. Have some crisp **iceberg lettuce leaves** washed and rinsed to roll up the tasty stir-fry.

polenta is also used in a recipe on page...
65.

polenta

baked polenta pie

Have your oven hot and ready at 180°C (350°F/Gas 4). Lightly grease a round ovenproof dish, no larger than 20 cm (8 inches) across, and sprinkle with 1 tablespoon instant polenta. Combine 75 g (2¹/₂ oz/¹/₂ cup) instant polenta, 250 ml (9 fl oz/1 cup) water, 3 tablespoons self-raising flour, 50 g (1³/₄ oz/¹/₂ cup) grated parmesan, 1 handful flat-leaf (Italian) parsley, chopped, and a good squeeze of lemon juice in a bowl, stirring to combine really well and spoon into the dish. Bake for 30 minutes. Allow to cool a little before turning out and cutting into wedges to serve as a substitute for mashed potato. Leftover pie can also be sliced and pan-fried in hot oil until golden.

herbed chicken schnitzel

Cut 2 skinless, boneless chicken breasts through the middle to give 4 thinner pieces. Put the chicken between 2 layers of plastic wrap and gently beat until 5 mm (¹/₄ inch) thick. Put 125 g (4¹/₂ oz/ 1 cup) well-seasoned flour in a bowl, 4 beaten eggs in another bowl and in a third bowl combine 150 g (5¹/₂ oz/1 cup) instant polenta, 50 g (1³/₄ oz/¹/₂ cup) grated parmesan and 2 teaspoons dried oregano. Dip the chicken in the flour, then in the beaten egg and, finally, press the chicken firmly into the herbed polenta mixture to evenly coat. Heat 250 ml (9 fl oz/ 1 cup) vegetable oil in a frying pan and cook the schnitzels in the hot, sizzling oil for 3–4 minutes each side. Serve with creamy mash.

tomato gratin

Have your oven hot and ready at 180°C (350°F/Gas 4). Cut 4 ripe and tasty tomatoes in half. Combine 3 tablespoons instant polenta, 1 teaspoon thyme leaves (or ¹/₂ teaspoon dried oregano) and a good seasoning of salt and black pepper in a bowl and press the cut side of the tomatoes firmly into the polenta mixture. Heat a splash of olive oil and 20 g (³/₄ oz) butter in a non-stick frying pan and cook the tomatoes, cut side down, for 3–4 minutes so they form a golden crust. Transfer to a baking tray, pour over any pan juices, sprinkle with 3 tablespoons grated parmesan and bake in the oven for 30 minutes, until the tomatoes are really soft and juicy.

red and brown lentils are also used in a recipe on page...
119.

red and brown lentils

lentil and bean curry

Cook 250 g (9 oz/1 cup) **red** or **brown lentils** in boiling water for 30 minutes and drain. Cook 1 chopped **onion** and 2 chopped **garlic cloves** in 40 g (1¹/2 oz) of sizzling **butter** for 2–3 minutes. Add 1 tablespoon **curry powder** and cook for 1 minute, to bring out the hidden spices in the powder. Add 400 g (14 oz) tinned **chopped tomatoes**, 500 ml (17 fl oz/2 cups) water and 3 handfuls trimmed and halved **green beans**, and boil. Cook on a rapid simmer for 10 minutes. Add the lentils and cook for a further 10 minutes, until thick and the lentils are really soft.

mediterranean lentil soup

Stir-fry 1 chopped **onion** and 1 chopped **garlic clove** in 60 g (2¹/4 oz) sizzling **butter** for a few minutes, to soften the onion. Add 250 g (9 oz/1 cup) **red** or **brown lentils**, 400 g (14 oz) tinned **chopped tomatoes**, 2 tablespoons **sun-dried tomato paste (concentrated purée)** and 750 ml (26 fl oz/3 cups) **chicken stock** to the pan and bring to the boil. Reduce the heat and simmer for 45 minutes, stirring often, until the lentils are soft and creamy. Serve with buttered fingers of toasted **Turkish (pide/flat) bread**.

chicken with spiced buttered lentils

Cook 125 g (4¹/2 oz/¹/2 cup) **red** or **brown lentils** in boiling water for 30 minutes and drain well. Put 1 chopped **onion**, 1 **garlic clove**, a 2 cm (³/4 inch) piece of **ginger** and 1 tablespoon **vegetable oil** in a food processor and blend to a smooth paste. Stir-fry 4 quartered **chicken thigh fillets** in a splash of hot **vegetable oil** for 5 minutes, until nicely browned. Add the onion mixture, 2 tablespoons **mild curry powder** and stir-fry for 5 minutes, to release all the hidden spices in the powder. Add the lentils, 1 chopped **carrot** and 500 ml (17 fl oz/2 cups) water to the pan and simmer for 15 minutes, until thickened. Stir through 40 g (1¹/2 oz) **butter** and a handful of chopped **coriander (cilantro) leaves** and cook on a gentle heat for 5 minutes. Serve with **basmati rice** and warm **naan bread**.

red curry paste is also used in recipes on pages...
75, 169 and 171.

red curry paste

spicy red chicken

Have your oven hot and ready at 180°C (350°F/Gas 4). Combine 2 tablespoons **red curry paste** in a bowl with 40 g (1 1/2 oz) **butter** and 6–8 finely chopped **basil leaves**. Rub this mixture under the skin of 4 **chicken breasts** (on the bone). Place the chicken on a baking tray and into the oven for 30 minutes. Serve the chicken with stir-fried **green beans** and **rice**.

fruity duck curry

Cook 125 ml (4 fl oz/1/2 cup) **coconut cream** in a saucepan over a high heat for 5–6 minutes, so little bubbling holes form and it starts to turn brown around the edge of the pan. Add 2 tablespoons **red curry paste** and stir-fry for 2 minutes. Add 2 tablespoons shaved **palm sugar** or **soft brown sugar** and stir-fry for 1 minute. Add 1 litre (35 fl oz/4 cups) **coconut milk** and bring to the boil. Add 1 **Chinese barbecued duck**, chopped into 10–12 pieces, to the pan with 250 g (9 oz) **cherry tomatoes**, 1 small handful **grapes**, 1 small handful **fresh** or **tinned lychees**, 80 g (2 3/4 oz/1/2 cup) chopped **pineapple** and a handful of **Thai basil**. Bring to the boil then reduce the heat to simmer for 10 minutes, to soften the fruit. Stir through 2 tablespoons **fish sauce** and serve with **rice**.

spicy thai lamb cutlets with beans and basil

Heat 3 tablespoons **vegetable oil** in a large frying pan. Cook 2 handfuls trimmed and halved **green beans** and stir-fry for 2 minutes, then set aside. Cook 12 **lamb cutlets**, in two batches, in the hot oil for 1 minute each side. Remove the lamb and drain all but 1 tablespoon of oil from the pan. Stir-fry 1 tablespoon **red curry paste** and 2 chopped **garlic cloves** for 1 minute. Add 125 ml (4 fl oz/1/2 cup) water, 1 tablespoon **sugar** and 2 tablespoons **fish sauce** and stir-fry until the paste is smooth and well-combined, then boil the sauce for 2–3 minutes. Return the beans and lamb to the pan with a handful of torn **Thai basil** and 4 torn **makrut (kaffir lime) leaves** and simmer for 5 minutes, turning the cutlets over in the pan, to coat in the sauce. Serve with **jasmine rice**.

red wine is also used in recipes on pages...

13, 131 and 203.

red wine

red wine and beef casserole

Have your oven hot and ready at 180°C (350°F/Gas 4). Cut 600 g (1 lb 5 oz) **chuck** or **stewing steak** into large cubes and put in a bowl with 60 g (2^1/$_4$ oz/^{1}/$_2$ cup) **plain (all-purpose) flour** and **salt** and **black pepper**. Toss the beef cubes around to coat in the flour. Heat a splash of **olive oil** and 20 g (^{3}/$_4$ oz) **butter** in a casserole dish and cook the beef in batches, so the meat sizzles and browns in the pan. Put the browned meat aside. Add 1 chopped **onion** and 2 chopped **bacon slices** to the pan and cook for 5 minutes, so the onion gently sizzles in the pan. Return the meat to the pan with 250 ml (9 fl oz/ 1 cup) **red wine**, 400 g (14 oz) tinned **chopped tomatoes**, 125 ml (4 fl oz/^{1}/$_2$ cup) water, 90 g (3^1/$_4$ oz/1 cup) chopped **button mushrooms** and 1 **bay leaf**. Cook in the oven for 1^1/$_2$ hours and serve with **potato mash**.

slow-cooked octopus in red wine, tomato and olive sauce

Put 2 chopped **small onions** and 2 **garlic cloves** in a food processor with 3 tablespoons good **olive oil** and process to a smooth paste. Put in a heavy-based saucepan with 250 ml (9 fl oz/1 cup) **red wine**, 400 g (14 oz) tinned **chopped tomatoes**, a handful of **small black olives** and a handful of roughly chopped **flat-leaf (Italian) parsley** and bring to the boil. Add 8 cleaned **small octopus** (cut the tentacles in half if too big), reduce the heat to low and simmer for 1 hour.

red wine and vanilla figs

Pour 250 ml (9 fl oz/1 cup) **red wine** into a saucepan. Split a **vanilla bean** and scape out the seeds. Add the seeds and the bean pod to the saucepan along with 110 g (3^3/$_4$ oz/^{1}/$_2$ cup) **sugar**, and boil for 5 minutes. Add 4 **figs**, simmer for 2–3 minutes then place on a lid and turn off the heat. Let the figs sit in the vanilla wine for 10 minutes. Eat the figs warm or at room temperature with **cream** or **ice cream**. Stored in the fridge overnight, the figs will have a more intense flavour.

red wine vinegar is also used in recipes on pages...
17, 63, 65, 103, 111, 123, 131, 207 and 213.

red wine vinegar

avocado and crispy prosciutto salad

Combine 1 crushed garlic clove, 1 teaspoon mustard, 3 tablespoons olive oil and 2 tablespoons red wine vinegar in a small bowl and whisk to combine. Heat a generous splash of olive oil in a non-stick frying pan and cook 6–8 slices of prosciutto for 2–3 minutes each side, until crispy. Put the prosciutto and any of the tasty oil from the pan in a large bowl with 2 avocados, cut into thick wedges, a handful of roasted capsicum (peppers), torn into strips, and 3 large handfuls baby rocket (arugula) or English spinach leaves. Pour over the dressing, gently toss to combine the ingredients and serve.

herbed caponata

Cook 1 finely cubed eggplant (aubergine) in 3 tablespoons hot olive oil until dark golden, stirring often so the eggplant cooks evenly. Add 1 diced red capsicum (pepper) and 2 chopped celery stalks, and cook for a minute, so the celery stays a little crunchy. Add 2 chopped anchovy fillets, 1 tablespoon rinsed capers, 110 g (3 3/4 oz/ 1/2 cup) chopped green olives, 2 tablespoons tomato paste (concentrated purée), 3 tablespoons red wine vinegar and 2 teaspoons sugar, and cook for 5 minutes. Stir through a handful of roughly chopped mint. Toss through your favourite pasta, add to bruschetta or serve as a side to grilled lamb.

sicilian chicken and pine nut pasta salad

Cook 400 g (14 oz) very small pasta (try orzo or risoni) in boiling water until al dente (different varieties require different cooking times). Drain well and add a little splash of olive oil to the pasta, tossing through with your hands so they stay separated, and allow to cool. Cook 1 finely sliced red capsicum (pepper) in a splash of olive oil in a saucepan for a couple of minutes then add 3 tablespoons red wine vinegar and 1 tablespoon soft brown sugar. Place on a lid and cook over a low heat for 5 minutes. Add to the pasta 350 g (12 oz/2 cups) shredded smoked chicken, 3 tablespoons lightly toasted pine nuts, 1 large handful roughly chopped flat-leaf (Italian) parsley and 60 g (2 1/4 oz/ 1/2 cup) sultanas (golden raisins). Toss to combine, season well and serve.

rice wine is also used in recipes on pages...
87, 155 and 165.

rice wine

sweet soy chicken wings

Cut the tips off 8 **chicken wings** and discard. Cut between the middle joint to give 16 perfect finger-food pieces. Heat 250 ml (9 fl oz/1 cup) **vegetable oil** in a wok. When the surface of the oil shimmers, carefully add a handful of the chicken and fry for 5 minutes, turning often so the pieces golden evenly. Remove to some paper towel and repeat, reheating the oil between each batch. Discard the oil and return all the chicken to the wok with 125 ml (4 fl oz/^{1}/$_2$ cup) **rice wine**, 125 ml (4 fl oz/^{1}/$_2$ cup) **chicken stock**, 2 chopped **garlic cloves**, a few thick slices of **ginger**, 3 tablespoons **dark soy sauce** and 3 tablespoons **soft brown sugar**. Bring to a rapid boil then reduce the heat to low and cover with a lid for 8–10 minutes. Remove the lid and increase the heat. Gently stir-fry for 2–3 minutes until the liquid becomes a thick, dark, sweet syrup coating the chicken.

black bean pork and broccoli hotpot

Cut 2 **pork fillets** into bite-sized cubes and toss around in a bowl with 4 tablespoons **black bean sauce**. Heat 2 tablespoons **light cooking oil** in a really hot casserole dish. Stir-fry 4 **spring onions (scallions)**, chopped into 3 cm (1^1/$_4$ inch) lengths, for a few seconds in the hot oil. Add the pork mixture to the wok and vigorously stir-fry for 4–5 minutes, to evenly brown the pork. Dissolve 2 teaspoons **cornflour (cornstarch)** in 125 ml (4 fl oz/^{1}/$_2$ cup) **rice wine** and pour into the pan with 125 ml (4 fl oz/^{1}/$_2$ cup) **chicken stock**, 1 tablespoon **oyster sauce** and a good pinch of **sugar**. Bring to the boil then add 120 g (4^1/$_4$ oz/2 cups) **broccoli florets**. Cover with a lid and cook over a low heat for 5 minutes. Serve over **rice**.

drunken chicken

Put 2 **skinless, boneless large chicken breasts** in a saucepan with 500 ml (17 fl oz/2 cups) **rice wine**, 1 tablespoon **salt** and a few thick slices of **ginger**. Add enough water so the chicken is covered and put on a medium heat. As soon as the stock boils, cover the pan with a tight-fitting lid, turn off the heat and set aside for 20 minutes. Remove the chicken and rest for 5 minutes. Thinly slice the chicken, top with a handful of roughly chopped **coriander (cilantro) leaves** and serve with steamed Asian greens, **rice** and **soy sauce** on the side.

salmon is also used in a recipe on page...
67.

salmon

three ways with

salmon shepherd's pie

Have your oven hot and ready at 180°C (350°F/Gas 4). Cook 1 chopped onion, 1 tablespoon rinsed small capers and 2 tablespoons finely chopped flat-leaf (Italian) parsley in 60 g (2¼ oz) hot sizzling butter for a few minutes until softened. Add 2 tablespoons plain (all-purpose) flour and stir for a minute over a gentle heat until a thick paste is formed. Slowly add 500 ml (17 fl oz/2 cups) milk, stirring constantly for a smooth, thick sauce. Stir through 500 g (1 lb 2 oz) tinned salmon, drained well and left in chunky pieces. Spoon into a baking dish. Cook 4 chopped all-purpose large potatoes in boiling water for 20 minutes. Drain and return to the pan with 40 g (1½ oz) butter and 3 tablespoons milk and mash until smooth. Spoon over the salmon and bake for 30 minutes.

salmon, potato and dill cakes

Cook 3 chopped all-purpose potatoes in boiling water for 10 minutes. Drain and roughly mash, leaving it a bit lumpy. Add 225 g (8 oz) tinned salmon, drained well, 2 tablespoons chopped dill, 1 chopped small onion and 1 egg and season well with salt and black pepper. Divide the mixture into 8, then roll and flatten each into a disc. Dip into a bowl of plain (all-purpose) flour, then dip into a bowl of lightly beaten egg and finally dip into a bowl of breadcrumbs, pressing firmly to evenly coat in the crumbs. Cook the salmon cakes in 125 ml (4 fl oz/½ cup) hot vegetable oil for 3–4 minutes each side, so they sizzle. Serve with a herb and caper mayonnaise.

salmon omelette

Have your grill (broiler) hot and ready. Beat 3 eggs and a splash of water in a bowl. Roughly mash 85 g (3 oz) tinned salmon, drained well, and add to the egg with a squeeze of lemon juice, 1 handful flat-leaf (Italian) parsley, chopped, and 3 tablespoons grated cheddar. Heat a little butter in a non-stick frying pan. Swirl the pan around to coat in the sizzling butter. Pour in the mixture and cook over a medium heat for 4–5 minutes, so the edges puff up and the bottom turns golden. Place under the grill until puffed up and golden on top. Grind over some black pepper and serve with toast. Serves 1.

sesame seeds are also used in recipes on pages...
29, 97, 135, 201 and 209.

sesame seeds

korean sesame barbecue marinade

Combine 1 tablespoon **sesame seeds** in a ceramic dish with 3 tablespoons **barbecue sauce**, 1 tablespoon **balsamic vinegar**, 2 finely chopped **spring onions (scallions)**, 1 teaspoon grated **ginger**, 1 crushed **garlic clove** and 1/4 teaspoon **chilli powder**. Add your meat and toss around to evenly coat in the marinade. Refrigerate for a few hours or overnight. Remove from the fridge 30 minutes before cooking to your liking on a hot grill or barbecue.

sesame-crusted tuna steaks with wasabi mayonnaise

Put 80 g (2 3/4 oz / 1/2 cup) **sesame seeds** on a plate. Press 4 **tuna steaks**, about 180–200 g (6 1/2 – 7 oz) each, firmly onto the seeds so they evenly coat the fish. Heat a few splashes of **light olive oil** in a hot non-stick frying pan and cook the tuna for 2–3 minutes each side, so they sizzle in the pan and turn the seeds a dark golden colour. Remove from the pan. Combine 125 g (4 1/2 oz / 1/2 cup) **mayonnaise** with 2 teaspoons **wasabi paste**, 1 crushed **garlic clove** and 1 teaspoon **tamari** or **soy sauce**. Serve the mayonnaise with the tuna and **potato mash** or **salad** on the side.

spicy sesame chicken salad

Put 2 teaspoons each **sesame seeds** and **sichuan peppercorns** in a hot, dry frying pan and shake the pan over the heat until the sesame seeds turn an even golden and the peppercorns start to smoke. Remove and allow to cool. Put the mixture in a food processor (or use a mortar and pestle) with 1 teaspoon **chilli flakes**, 2 tablespoons **light soy sauce**, 2 teaspoons **sesame oil** and 1 teaspoon **caster (superfine) sugar** and blend to a paste. Shred the skin and meat of a **barbecued chicken** and toss around in a bowl with 1 sliced **Lebanese (short) cucumber** and 4 finely sliced **spring onions (scallions)**. Add the paste and toss well to evenly coat the chicken in the spicy dressing.

Peso Netto **1000** g e

RISO VIALONE NANO

SEMI INTEGRALE

SEMI INTEGRALE

Riccò R.
Isola della Scala
(VR) via Verona n° 46
Tel. 045/7300601

Da consumarsi preferibilmente entro il:

short-grain rice is also used in recipes on pages...
21, 55 and 159.

short-grain rice

baked tuna and zucchini risotto

Have your oven hot and ready at 200°C (400°F/Gas 6). Heat a splash of **olive oil** in a casserole dish and stir-fry 1 chopped **onion** and 2 grated **zucchini (courgettes)** for 2–3 minutes, so the onion softens and sizzles in the hot oil. Add 220 g (7³/₄ oz/1 cup) **short-grain rice** to the pan, stir for a minute then add 225 g (8 oz) tinned **tuna**, drained, 400 g (14 oz) tinned **chopped tomatoes**, 1 teaspoon **rosemary leaves**, 375 ml (13 fl oz/ 1¹/₂ cups) **chicken stock** and season well with **sea salt** and **black pepper**. Bring to the boil, cover the dish with a tight-fitting lid and cook in the oven for 30 minutes. Scatter a handful of chopped **flat-leaf (Italian) parsley** on top. Serves 2.

niçoise rice salad

Cook 220 g (7³/₄ oz/1 cup) **short-grain rice** in boiling water for 12–15 minutes, so the grains are still slightly firm in the centre. Rinse, drain well and put in a bowl with 225 g (8 oz) tinned **tuna** (add the tasty oil from the tin), 2 finely chopped **anchovy fillets**, 2 chopped firm **tomatoes**, 2 quartered **hard-boiled eggs**, 1 small handful **flat-leaf (Italian) parsley**, finely chopped, 2 tablespoons finely chopped **chives** and 3 tablespoons **black olives**. Gently toss to combine, being careful not to break up the eggs too much. Season well with **salt** and **black pepper** and serve with **lemon wedges** on the side. Serves 2.

baked vanilla rice pudding

Have your oven hot and ready at 160°C (315°F/Gas 2–3). Rub a little **butter** to grease the inside of a 1 litre (35 fl oz/4 cup) baking dish. Combine 750 ml (26 fl oz/3 cups) **milk**, 3 tablespoons **sugar**, 3 eggs and 1 teaspoon **natural vanilla extract** in a bowl. Beat until the eggs are just combined then pour into the prepared dish. Sprinkle 3 tablespoons **short-grain rice** into the custard mixture, sprinkle with a little **ground nutmeg** and bake for 50 minutes. Serve with **cherry** or **fig jam** and **cream**. Serves 4–6.

short pasta is also used in recipes on pages...
13, 19, 23, 37, 49, 71, 81, 91, 173, 183 and 207.

short pasta

springtime minestrone

Cook 90 g (3¼ oz/1 cup) small shell pasta in boiling water for 8–10 minutes. Heat a splash of olive oil in a saucepan and cook 1 chopped onion and 1 thyme sprig for 5 minutes, so the onion sizzles and softens. Add 1 chopped garlic clove, 1 chopped small carrot, 2 chopped celery stalks and 2 chopped zucchini (courgettes) and cook for 3–4 minutes. Add 1.5 litres (52 fl oz/6 cups) chicken stock and bring to the boil for 15 minutes. Add the pasta to the soup, season well and stir through a handful of chopped flat-leaf (Italian) parsley. Simmer for 5 minutes. Serve topped with some finely grated parmesan.

penne with italian sausage, basil and pecorino

Remove the skin from 4 Italian sausages and roughly chop the meat. Cook 400 g (14 oz) penne for 8–10 minutes in boiling water. Drain and return to the pan. Heat a splash of good olive oil in a large saucepan and cook 1 chopped onion for a few minutes. Add the sausage meat to the pan and stir-fry for 5 minutes, until browned. Add 400 g (14 oz) tinned chopped tomatoes, 1 handful torn basil, 125 ml (4 fl oz/½ cup) water and a pinch each of sugar and salt. Boil for 5 minutes then stir through the pasta and 45 g (1½ oz/½ cup) grated pecorino.

chilli pumpkin rigatoni

Cook 400 g (14 oz) rigatoni in boiling water for 8 minutes then drain well. Heat 3 tablespoons light olive oil in a frying pan and add 300 g (10½ oz/2 cups) peeled and cubed pumpkin (winter squash) pieces, 1 chopped large red chilli and 2 chopped garlic cloves. Stir-fry over a high heat for 2 minutes. Reduce the heat to low, cover and cook for 10 minutes. Stir a few times, then cover and cook for another 4–5 minutes. Put the cooked pumpkin mixture and any oil from the pan in a large bowl with the rigatoni, 1 tablespoon lemon juice, 50 g (1¾ oz/½ cup) grated parmesan and 2 handfuls mizuna. Season with salt and black pepper, toss to combine and serve warm.

soy sauce is also used in recipes on pages...

15, 17, 29, 33, 51, 65, 87, 93, 95, 97, 109, 125, 127, 133, 135, 145, 147, 153, 155, 165, 173, 185, 189, 197, 201 and 211.

soy sauce

red braised pork fillet

Combine 1 litre (35 fl oz/4 cups) chicken stock, 125 ml (4 fl oz/ 1/2 cup) light soy sauce, 2 tablespoons dark soy sauce, 1 teaspoon five-spice, 95 g (3 1/4 oz/ 1/2 cup) soft brown sugar, 2 garlic cloves and 4–6 thick slices of ginger in a saucepan and boil for 5 minutes. Add 2 pork fillets, reduce the heat to low and cover for 20 minutes, turning the pork halfway through the cooking time. Remove, cover the pork with foil and allow to rest for 5 minutes. Slice and serve with rice or noodles, steamed Asian greens and some of the hot braising liquid spooned over the top.

soy-simmered vegetables with tofu

Boil 750 ml (26 fl oz/3 cups) chicken stock, 3 tablespoons light soy sauce and 2 tablespoons mirin (or 2 teaspoons sugar) in a frying pan. Add 450 g (1 lb/3 cups) peeled and cubed pumpkin (winter squash), 1 chopped carrot, 100 g (3 1/2 oz) shiitake mushrooms and 4 spring onions (scallions), cut into 3 cm (1 1/4 inch) lengths, to the pan. Simmer the vegetables for 10 minutes, turning often. Add 300 g (10 1/2 oz) firm tofu, cut into 2 cm (3/4 in) cubes, and cook for a further 5 minutes. Serve with rice.

ginger teriyaki chicken

Toss 4–6 chicken thigh fillets around in a bowl with 125 ml (4 fl oz/ 1/2 cup) chicken stock, 3 tablespoons light soy sauce, 2 teaspoons finely grated ginger and a heaped teaspoon of sugar. Marinate for a few hours if you have the time, otherwise heat a grill (barbecue) plate to smoking hot. Shake the excess marinade off the chicken and cook for 5 minutes each side. Quickly boil the marinade for a few minutes, slice the chicken and serve on rice with the hot sauce over and sprinkled with some chilli powder.

stale bread is also used in a recipe on page...
105.

stale bread

three ways with

pasta with chilli crumbs

Cook 400 g (14 oz) **spaghetti** in boiling water for 8–10 minutes. Meanwhile, heat a few splashes of **olive oil** in a frying pan and cook 100 g (3 1/2 oz/1 cup) **breadcrumbs** (stale sourdough makes delicious crumbs) for a few minutes until they start to turn crispy golden. Put in a bowl. Add a few more splashes of **oil** to the pan and cook 3 chopped **garlic cloves**, 1 teaspoon **chilli flakes** and 4–6 chopped **anchovy fillets** and stir-fry for 2 minutes, to flavour the oil. Add the cooked pasta to the pan with the crumbs, 50 g (1 3/4 oz/ 1/2 cup) grated **parmesan**, a handful of **flat-leaf (Italian) parsley**, roughly chopped, and a good grinding of **black pepper**. Toss around well to combine the ingredients and serve.

crumbed prawns with plum sauce

Place a peeled and deveined **raw large prawn (shrimp)** between 2 layers of plastic wrap and gently pound to flatten. Repeat to make 12 prawn cutlets. Put 2 tablespoons **cornflour (cornstarch)**, 2 beaten **eggs** and 100 g (3 1/2 oz/1 cup) **breadcrumbs** (made with stale bread) in three separate bowls. Toss each prawn in the cornflour, dip into the egg then gently press into the crumbs. Fill a wok one-third full with **vegetable oil** over a medium heat. When the surface of the oil is shimmering, cook the prawns in 2 batches for 2–3 minutes, so the breadcrumbs turn dark golden. Serve with **plum sauce** or 2 tablespoons **light soy sauce** mixed with 1 tablespoon **lemon juice**.

parmesan and herb crumbed lamb cutlets

Whiz-up some **stale bread** in a food processor to make about 200 g (7 oz/2 cups) **breadcrumbs**. Put the crumbs in a bowl, 3 beaten **eggs** in another bowl, and 100 g (3 1/2 oz/1 cup) grated **parmesan** mixed with 1 teaspoon **dried oregano** in a third. Working one at a time, dip a trimmed **lamb cutlet** in the flour, then in the egg then in the herbed parmesan, pressing firmly onto the lamb to coat in the parmesan. Repeat to make 12 cutlets. Heat a few splashes of **light olive oil** in a non-stick frying pan and cook the lamb in batches, over a medium heat, for 3–4 minutes each side, until they look deliciously golden and crispy. Serve with **potato mash** and **beans**.

sweet chilli sauce

sticky chilli lime ribs

Cook 16 **American-style pork ribs** in boiling water for 10 minutes. Drain and allow to cool. Combine 250 ml (9 fl oz/1 cup) **chicken stock**, 3 tablespoons **sweet chilli sauce**, 2 tablespoons **lime juice**, 1 teaspoon grated **lime zest** and 2 tablespoons **fish sauce** in a bowl. Heat a splash of **cooking oil** in a really hot wok. Add the ribs and stir-fry for 3–4 minutes. Add the sauce and boil for 8–10 minutes, until the sticky sauce thickly coats the ribs.

barbecued duck rice salad

Heat 2 tablespoons **vegetable oil** in a saucepan. When the oil is just about smoking hot, add 400 g (14 oz/2 cups) **jasmine rice** and stir for 2 minutes, so the rice turns lightly golden and smells nutty. Add 750 ml (26 fl oz/3 cups) **chicken stock** (it will splutter in the pan). As soon as the stock boils, place on a tight-fitting lid and cook on a really low heat for 25 minutes. Remove from the heat, stir a few times and put in a large bowl and allow to cool. Add 1 shredded **Chinese barbecued duck** (or a **barbecued chicken**) to the rice with 125 ml (4 fl oz/ 1/2 cup) **sweet chilli sauce**, 1 finely sliced **small red onion**, 1 finely sliced **Lebanese (short) cucumber** and 1 large handful each roughly chopped **coriander (cilantro) leaves** and **mint**. Toss together well and serve.

chargrilled chilli prawns

Put 125 ml (4 fl oz/1/2 cup) **sweet chilli sauce** in a bowl with 1 teaspoon **ground cumin**, 2 tablespoons finely chopped **coriander (cilantro) leaves and stems** and 1/2 teaspoon **white pepper**. Add 16 peeled and deveined **raw large prawns (shrimp)**, tossing around to coat in the marinade. Cover and refrigerate for 30 minutes, or a few hours if you have the time. Heat a little oil on a smoking-hot chargrill or barbecue hotplate and cook the prawns for 3 minutes each side. Remove and squeeze over some **lime juice** and season with **sea salt**. Serve with **salad**, **wedges** or **mash**.

طحينة فاخرة

المحتويات ١٠٠٪ سمسم معصور

طرابلس - لبنان - شارع سوريا - هاتف ٨ - ٣٨١١٨٧-٦

Kalaajieh

Established 1877

Tahine Extra

Contains 100% Seasame Seeds Crush

Tripoli - Lebanon - Syria street - Tel. 06-381187-8

Serving Size		
Amount per Serving		
Calories 200	Ca	
Total Fat 16g		
Sodium 10mg		
Total Carbohydrate		
Protein 9g		
Shake well		

IMPORTED
KHALI
214 - THE B
PUNCHBOW
Tel 02 - 7

قلعجية

تأسست عام ١٨٧٧

طحينة فاخرة

tahini is also used in a recipe on page...
57.

tahini

roast pumpkin, tahini and couscous salad

Have your oven hot and ready at 180°C (350°F/Gas 4). Toss 300 g (10 1/2 oz/2 cups) peeled and cubed **pumpkin (winter squash)** in a bowl with a splash of **olive oil**, 1 teaspoon each **ground cumin** and **sea salt**, and a good grinding of **black pepper**. You can also add a pinch of **chilli flakes** or some chopped **fresh chilli** if you like. Place the pumpkin pieces on a baking tray and roast for 30 minutes. Meanwhile, combine 135 g (4 3/4 oz/1/2 cup) **tahini**, 2 tablespoons **lemon juice**, 2 crushed **garlic cloves** and 1 teaspoon **sea salt** and stir until smooth. Toss the cooked pumpkin with 2–3 handfuls **baby rocket (arugula) leaves** and spoon over the dressing. Serve with **steamed couscous**.

fried cauliflower with lemon tahini

Whiz-up 3 tablespoons **tahini** in a food processor with 250 g (9 oz/ 1 cup) **Greek-style yoghurt**, 1 teaspoon **ground cumin**, 1 crushed **garlic clove** and 2 tablespoons **lemon juice** until you have a smooth sauce. Season well with **sea salt**. Heat 500 ml (17 fl oz/2 cups) **vegetable oil** in a frying pan so the surface of the oil is gently shimmering. Break large florets off a small head of **cauliflower** and cook several pieces at a time in the oil, turning often until they are golden brown all over. Repeat with the remaining cauliflower florets and serve with the sauce.

bang bang chicken salad

Combine 2 tablespoons **tahini** in a bowl with 1 teaspoon **sesame oil**, 2 tablespoons **light soy sauce** and 1 tablespoon **balsamic** or **Chinese black vinegar**. Toss the shredded meat and skin of a **barbecued chicken** in a bowl with 2 sliced **cucumbers** and 3 sliced **spring onions (scallions)**. Pour over the sauce, gently toss and serve the salad on several leaves of **butter** or **mignonette lettuce**. Sprinkle with 2 teaspoons lightly toasted **sesame seeds**.

tomatoes are also used in recipes on pages...
13, 25, 55, 81, 89, 95, 99, 103, 111, 117, 119, 131, 137, 143,
177, 181, 193, 207 and 215.

tomatoes

three ways with

ginger tomato fish stew with coriander rice

Cook 400 g (14 oz/2 cups) long-grain rice in boiling water for 10–12 minutes. Drain well and stir through 1 handful coriander (cilantro) leaves, finely chopped. Meanwhile, put 1 chopped onion, 2 garlic cloves and 1 tablespoon grated ginger in a food processor and whiz to a smooth paste. Heat a splash of vegetable oil in a saucepan and cook the paste for 5 minutes over a gentle heat until fragrant. Add 400 g (14 oz) tinned chopped tomatoes, 125 ml (4 fl oz/1/2 cup) water and boil for 5 minutes. Add 2 cubed white fish fillets, stir once and cover. Cook over a gentle heat for 10 minutes. Season well with sea salt and black pepper and serve with the coriander rice.

lamb and rosemary ragout

Cook 1 chopped onion, 1 chopped garlic clove and 1 tablespoon rosemary needles in a splash of olive oil for a few minutes, so the onion gently softens in the oil. Add 500 g (1 lb 2 oz) cubed lamb shoulder, 400 g (14 oz) tinned chopped tomatoes and 250 ml (9 fl oz/1 cup) each red wine and water. Bring to the boil and simmer on a gentle heat for 1 1/2 hours, stirring often, until the lamb is really tender. Season well and serve with potato mash, risoni or soft polenta.

roasted tomato pasta sauce

Have your oven hot and ready at 180°C (350°F/Gas 4). Put 800 g (1 lb 12 oz) tinned tomatoes in a baking tray with 1 quartered onion, 2 chopped garlic cloves and a good pinch of sea salt and sugar. If you want, add a pinch of bicarbonate of soda (baking soda) to help neutralize the sometimes acidic taste of tinned tomatoes. Cook in the oven for 1 hour. Whiz the mixture in a food processor with a handful of basil. Toss through your favourite pasta and serve with lots of grated parmesan. Pouring (whipping) cream can be added to make soup, and the sauce can be used as a base for pizzas.

tomato passata is also used in recipes on pages...
37, 39, 71 and 209.

tomato passata

creamy tomato and basil soup

Cook 1 chopped **garlic clove** and 1 chopped **onion** in 20 g (³/₄ oz) sizzling **butter** for 3–4 minutes, to soften the onions. Add 750 ml (26 fl oz/3 cups) **tomato passata (puréed tomatoes)** and a handful of **basil** to the pan. Bring to the boil and simmer for a couple of minutes. Pour into a food processor and blend until smooth. Return to the saucepan and stir through 125 ml (4 fl oz/½ cup) **thickened (whipping) cream** and season well with **salt** and **black pepper**. Serve with **toast** sprinkled with **parmesan** and grilled until golden.

pappardelle with anchovies and tomato cream sauce

Cook 400 g (14 oz) **pappardelle** in boiling water for 8–10 minutes. Drain well and return to the warm saucepan. Meanwhile, heat a few splashes of good **fruity olive oil** in a saucepan with 3–4 **anchovy fillets** and sizzle the anchovies over a gentle heat so they break up and flavour the oil. Add 3 chopped **garlic cloves** and stir-fry for a minute (don't burn it) and add 250 ml (9 fl oz/1 cup) **tomato passata (puréed tomatoes)**. Simmer for 10 minutes and add 3 tablespoons **pouring (whipping) cream**. Toss through the pasta and top with grated **parmesan**.

poppy seed and lime chicken curry

Heat a splash of **vegetable oil** in a frying pan and cook 4 **chicken thigh fillets**, cut into large bite-sized pieces, for 4–5 minutes until golden. Remove from the pan. Add 1 chopped **onion**, 8–10 **curry leaves**, 1 tablespoon **poppy seeds** and a good grinding of **black pepper** to the pan and stir-fry for 2–3 minutes, so the onion sizzles and browns in the hot oil. Add 2 tablespoons **mild Indian curry paste**, stir-fry for 2–3 minutes then return the chicken to the pan with 500 ml (17 fl oz/2 cups) **tomato passata (puréed tomatoes)** and 250 ml (9 fl oz/1 cup) water. Bring to the boil, then reduce the heat to a rapid simmer for 30 minutes. Stir through 3 tablespoons **lime juice** and a handful of roughly chopped **coriander (cilantro) leaves**.

tuna is also used in recipes on pages...
19, 23, 105 and 191.

tuna

tuna and eggplant rigatoni

Cook 400 g (14 oz) **rigatoni** in boiling water for 8–10 minutes. Drain and return to the pan. Meanwhile, heat a few tablespoons of **olive oil** in a frying pan and sizzle 1 **small eggplant (aubergine)**, chopped into 2 cm ($^3/4$ inch) cubes, in the hot oil until golden. Add $^1/2$ teaspoon **dried oregano**, 400 g (14 oz) tinned **chopped tomatoes** and 125 ml (4 fl oz/ $^1/2$ cup) water and simmer rapidly for 8–10 minutes. Stir through 370 g (13 oz) tinned **tuna**, drained of excess oil, and a handful of **black olives**. Stir through to warm but don't break up the tuna too much. Add to the pasta, toss together and serve.

tapas tuna salad

Cook 6 thickly sliced **small boiling potatoes** (try nicola) in boiling water for 8–10 minutes. Add 175 g (6 oz) **asparagus**, cut in half and with woody ends trimmed, to the water for 1 minute. Rinse the vegetables under cold water and drain well. Toss the potato and asparagus in a bowl with 450 g (1 lb) tinned **tuna**, drained of excess oil, a handful of **green olives**, $^1/2$ teaspoon **chilli flakes**, 1 sliced **small red onion** and 2 tablespoons good **olive oil**. Sprinkle over $^1/2$ teaspoon **smoked paprika** and serve with some **lemon wedges** on the side.

tuna fattoush

Have your oven hot and ready at 220°C (425°F/Gas 7). Tear up 2 pieces of **lavash** (or other unleavened bread) into bite-sized pieces, place on a tray and into the oven for 10 minutes, turning once, until crispy. Gently toss together 2 chopped **Lebanese (short) cucumbers**, 2 chopped ripe and tasty **tomatoes**, 4 sliced **spring onions (scallions)**, 1 handful each **black olives** and **mint**, 2 tablespoons **olive oil** and 1 tablespoon **red wine vinegar**. Add the toasted bread and 375 g (13 oz) tinned **tuna**, drained of excess oil, and gently toss (don't break up the tuna too much). Grind some **black pepper** over the top or, if you have some in your pantry, sprinkle over 2 teaspoons **sumac** instead.

turkish bread

cheat's pizza

Have your oven hot and ready at 220°C (425°F/Gas 7). Cut a 20 cm (8 inch) piece of Turkish (pide/flat) bread in half to give two thinner pieces and spread with 3 tablespoons tomato passata (puréed tomatoes) and 2 tablespoons basil pesto over each. Top each with a handful of sliced leg ham, 6 small pitted black olives, 1 sliced large bocconcini ball (fresh baby mozzarella), a sprinkling of dried oregano and the slightest drizzle of olive oil. Put on a baking tray and blast in the oven for 10 minutes.

toasty spiced fingers

Lightly toast 2 tablespoons sesame seeds in a frying pan until golden and aromatic, shaking the pan all the time so they cook evenly. Add 2 teaspoons dried oregano, 2 teaspoons chopped thyme, 2 teaspoons sumac and 1 teaspoon sea salt. Shake the pan for a minute over a high heat and pour the spice mix into a bowl to cool. Cover until ready to use. Have your oven hot and ready at 220°C (425°F/Gas 7). Cut a 20 cm (8 inch) piece of Turkish (pide/flat) bread in half to give two thinner pieces, brush 3 tablespoons olive oil evenly over the bread and sprinkle 1 tablespoon of the spice mixture over each piece. Pop on a baking tray and into the oven for 5 minutes. Remove and allow to cool a bit before cutting into 3 cm (1¼ inch) slices to have dipped into soft-boiled eggs or on a Middle Eastern platter.

turkish fig pudding

Have your oven hot and ready at 200°C (400°F/Gas 6). Grease a 1–1.5 litre (35–52 fl oz/4–6 cup) ovenproof dish. Cut a 10 cm (4 inch) wide piece of Turkish (pide/flat) bread in half to give two thinner pieces and roughly tear into smaller bite-sized pieces. Combine 40 g (1½ oz) softened butter and 3 tablespoons fig jam in a bowl, spread over the pieces of bread and arrange them in the bottom of the dish. Combine 250 ml (9 fl oz/ 1 cup) pouring (whipping) cream, 250 ml (9 fl oz/1 cup) milk, 2 eggs and 115 g (4 oz/½ cup) caster (superfine) sugar in a bowl (if you have any rosewater, add 1 teaspoon here for a truly Turkish experience), pour over the bread and cook in the oven for 30 minutes.

udon noodles

ginger teriyaki eggplant

Cook 300 g (10½ oz) **dried udon noodles** in boiling water for 4–5 minutes and drain well. Combine 2 tablespoons **soy sauce** in a bowl with 250 ml (9 fl oz/ 1 cup) **chicken stock**, 2 teaspoons finely grated **ginger**, 1 crushed **garlic clove**, 1 teaspoon **sugar** and 1 teaspoon **sesame oil**. Slice an **eggplant (aubergine)** into 8 rounds. Heat 3 tablespoons **vegetable oil** in a hot wok or frying pan and cook the eggplant slices for 2 minutes each side. Remove the eggplant and drain all the oil from the wok. Pour in the sauce mixture. Bring to the boil then reduce the heat to a simmer for 2 minutes. Return the eggplant to the pan, tossing to coat in the sauce and cook for a further 2–3 minutes, until the sauce is thick and glossy. Add the noodles, gently tossing to coat in the eggplant and sauce. Serve sprinkled with 2 finely shredded **spring onions (scallions)** and **rice**.

duck and udon soup

Bring 1 litre (35 fl oz/4 cups) **chicken stock** to the boil. Finely shred the meat and skin of half a **Chinese barbecued duck**. Put the duck bones (this is where all the Chinese spice flavours hide) into the saucepan and cook for 5 minutes in the chicken stock. Strain, discard the bones, and return the stock to the pan. Now add the duck meat to the pan with 100 g (3½ oz) **shiitake mushrooms**, stems cut off, 2 handfuls chopped **Chinese greens** (try Chinese broccoli) and a few splashes of **soy sauce**. Meanwhile, cook 300 g (10½ oz) **dried udon noodles** in boiling water for 3–4 minutes. Drain and add to the duck soup. Serve with a drizzle of **sesame oil**.

five-spice chicken with buttered udon

Quarter 4 **chicken thigh fillets** and toss around in a bowl with 1 teaspoon **five-spice**, 2 teaspoons grated **ginger** and 2 tablespoons **soy sauce**. Set aside for 30 minutes. Heat a frying pan to high and add a splash of **cooking oil**. Add the chicken, shaking off and reserving any excess marinade, and stir-fry for a few minutes until well browned. Add the marinade to the pan with 250 ml (9 fl oz/1 cup) **chicken stock**. Bring to the boil, reduce the heat and simmer for 10 minutes. Cook 300 g (10½ oz) **dried udon noodles** in boiling water for 4–5 minutes. Add the noodles to the pan with 40 g (1½ oz) **butter**, toss around to evenly combine then serve.

walnuts are also used in recipes on pages...
21, 35 and 41.

walnuts

walnut, goat's cheese and bean salad

Cook 4 large handfuls **mixed beans** (try both green and yellow varieties) in boiling water for 2 minutes. Drain well. Heat a good few splashes of **olive oil** in a frying pan and cook 1 chopped **garlic clove** for a few seconds to flavour the oil. Add the beans to the pan and cook for a few minutes, to coat in the garlicky oil then add 2 tablespoons **red wine vinegar** to the pan. Stir around for a minute and add 1 small handful **flat-leaf (Italian) parsley**, chopped, and 60 g (2¼ oz/½ cup) crumbled **goat's cheese** to the pan with a good grinding of **black pepper**. Stir for a minute, until the goat's cheese is just starting to melt and serve with 60 g (2¼ oz/½ cup) lightly toasted chopped **walnuts** sprinkled over.

waldorf salad thai-style

Put the shredded meat from a **barbecued chicken** in a bowl with 1 large handful **coriander (cilantro) leaves and stems**, roughly chopped, 2 **green apples**, cut into thin strips, 2 finely sliced **celery stalks** and 100 g (3½ oz/1 cup) lightly toasted **walnuts**. Combine 250 g (9 oz/1 cup) **mayonnaise** with 2 tablespoons **fish sauce** and 1 tablespoon **lime juice** and add to the salad. Toss to evenly combine all the ingredients.

caramel walnut tart

Have your oven hot and ready at 220°C (425°F/Gas 7). Fold the edges of a sheet of **puff pastry** over to make a 1 cm (½ in) border. Place on a baking tray and cook in the oven for 10 minutes. Meanwhile, combine 2 tablespoons **thick (double/heavy) cream**, 40 g (1½ oz) **butter**, 3 tablespoons **soft brown sugar** and 3 tablespoons **honey** in a saucepan and cook over a gentle heat, stirring constantly, until the mixture looks like smooth caramel. Add 250 g (9 oz/2 cups) **walnuts** and stir to coat the walnuts in the caramel. Spoon evenly over the tart and cook in the oven for a further 10 minutes. Serve warm with **ice cream**.

white vinegar is also used in a recipe on page...
57.

white vinegar

easy hollandaise

Combine 3 **egg yolks** and
1 tablespoon **white vinegar** (but
even better if you have white wine
vinegar) in a food processor for
a few seconds. Heat 200 g (7 oz)
butter in a saucepan until it is
bubbling hot, being careful not to
burn it. With the motor running,
slowly pour the hot butter into the
food processor in a steady stream.
Remove to a bowl and set aside
for 10 minutes to thicken slightly.
Season well and serve over
poached eggs or **salmon fillets**,
with **chips (fries)** or **fillet steak**.

corn chips with jalapeño salsa

Roughly chop 4 firm **tomatoes**
and put in a food processor with
1 chopped **garlic clove**, 1 chopped
small red onion, 2 tablespoons
pickled jalapeño chillies and a
tablespoon of the **brine** from the
jar, 2 tablespoons **white vinegar**
and a good pinch of **salt**, **black
pepper** and **sugar**. Pulse to make
a thick, chunky sauce and put in
a bowl. Stir through 2 handfuls
coriander (cilantro) leaves, roughly
chopped, and enjoy with warm
and crispy **corn chips**.

south indian hot and sour prawn curry

Toss 16 peeled and deveined **raw
large prawns (shrimp)**, tails on,
in a bowl with 2 tablespoons **mild
Indian curry paste** (try madras
or balti) so the prawns are evenly
coated in the paste. Heat a few
splashes of **light olive oil** in a
frying pan and stir-fry the prawns
for 2–3 minutes over a medium
heat. Remove the prawns. Add a
little more **oil** to the pan and stir-
fry 1 sliced **onion** and 2 chopped
garlic cloves for 2–3 minutes over
a gentle heat. Add 400 g (14 oz)
tinned **chopped tomatoes**, stir to
combine and boil for 5 minutes, to
thicken a little. Return the prawns
to the pan with 2 tablespoons
white vinegar and cook for another
minute. Stir through 1 large
handful **coriander (cilantro) leaves**,
chopped, and serve with **basmati
rice** and some warm **naan bread**.

recipe index

C

thank you

Within a few minutes of discussing this book Kay Scarlett knew we were on to a good thing. Thank you Kay for that confidence and sharing the vision and enthusiasm.

Thank you to Juliet and the rest of the crew at Murdoch Books, a genuinely gorgeous bunch of people. Thanks especially to Viv and Paul for all their hard work. And to Brett, whose photography captured the spirit of this book.

My sister Sue and friend Mikey for coming over and being the most motivated, hands-on helpers/testers/food critics I could wish for. Good one guys and a big hug to both of you.

To BA. Thanks for the laptop rental.

And to Matt. Thanks for being so bloody supportive!

Ross x.

This edition published in Canada in 2007 by Whitecap Books, 351 Lynn Ave., North Vancouver, British Columbia, Canada, V7J 2C4
www.whitecap.ca

First published by Murdoch Books Pty Limited in 2007
www.murdochbooks.com.au

Chief executive: Juliet Rogers
Publisher: Kay Scarlett

Editor: Paul McNally
Design and art direction: Vivien Valk
Photography and styling: Brett Stevens
Props: Jo Briscoe
Production: Maiya Levitch
Colour reproduction: Splitting Image Colour Studio, Melbourne, Australia

Text copyright © Ross Dobson 2007
Design and photography copyright © Murdoch Books 2007

ISBN   1 55285 875 8
ISBN   978 1 55285 875 2

Printed by Midas Printing (Asia) Ltd. in 2007. Printed in China.

IMPORTANT: Those who might be at risk from the effects of salmonella poisoning (the elderly, pregnant women, young children and those suffering from immune deficiency diseases) should consult their doctor with any concerns about eating raw eggs.

CONVERSION GUIDE: You may find cooking times vary depending on the oven you are using. For fan-forced ovens, as a general rule, set the oven temperature to 20°C (35°F) lower than indicated in the recipe. We have used 20 ml (4 teaspoon) tablespoon measures. If you are using a 15 ml (3 teaspoon) tablespoon, for most recipes the difference will not be noticeable. However, for recipes using baking powder, gelatine, bicarbonate of soda (baking soda) or small amounts of cornflour (cornstarch), add an extra teaspoon for each tablespoon specified.